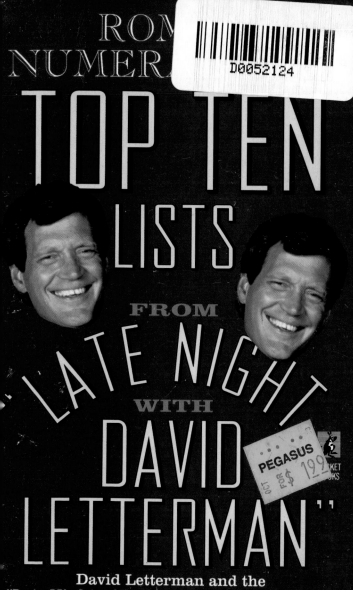

ROMAN
NUMERAL

TOP TEN
LISTS
FROM
"LATE NIGHT
WITH
DAVID
LETTERMAN"

David Letterman and the
"Late Night with David Letterman" Writers

D0052124

$5.99 U.S.
$7.50 CAN.

ISBN 0-671-51144-0

5 0 5 9 9 >

EAN

ROMAN NUMERAL TWO!

TOP TEN LISTS

FROM

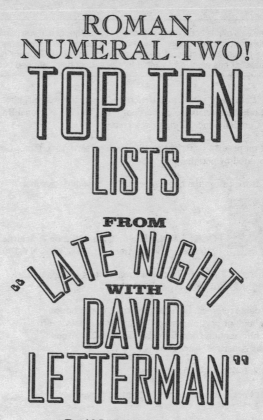

"LATE NIGHT WITH DAVID LETTERMAN"

David Letterman and the
"Late Night with David Letterman" Writers

POCKET BOOKS

New York   London   Toronto   Sydney   Tokyo   Singapore

All "Late Night with David Letterman" program excerpts, photographs and other materials are property of NBC, © 1991 National Broadcasting Company, Inc. All rights reserved.

List on page 14 copyright © 1991 by The New York Times Company. Reprinted by permission.

An excerpt from the book appeared in *Playboy* Magazine.

POCKET BOOKS, a division of Simon & Schuster Inc.
1230 Avenue of the Americas, New York, NY 10020

Copyright © 1991 by National Broadcasting Company, Inc.
and Cardboard Shoe Productions, Inc.

ISBN: 0-671-51144-0

First Pocket Books paperback printing November 1994

10 9 8 7 6 5 4 3 2 1

POCKET and colophon are registered trademarks of
Simon & Schuster Inc.

"Late Night With David Letterman" and "Late Night" are Service
Marks of the National Broadcasting Company, Inc.

Cover photo of David Letterman courtesy of The National Broadcasting
Company, Inc., © The National Broadcasting Company, Inc.

Printed in the U.S.A.

ACKNOWLEDGMENTS

Thanks to:

Sally Peters

Barbara Sheehan

Carol Collings

Carol Mark

Bea Clark

Ken Keeler, Ph.D.

Pami Shamir

And a special thanks to Mr. Rollins for letting us use all
the old lumber behind his garage.

FOREWORD

You'll get a kick out of this. The other night after dinner, I'm watching television, trying to relax at the end of a long, hard day. They're showing this program starring that very popular blond actress who plays a curvaceous college co-ed with a great deal of sex appeal who lives with six football players, all of whom have a romantic interest in her. The only reason the landlord lets these guys live there is because he believes they are actually mental patients—you know, insane—and she is their nurse or something. But of course it's all just pretend so they can stay there for really cheap rent. It's very comical. Anyway, I'm enjoying this program and all of a sudden my wife, Linda, says, "You pay more attention to that television actress than you do to me." Well now, frankly, this is old news. And that's exactly what I tell Linda. I say, "Linda, it's old news." And then I add the scorcher. I say, "You know, Linda, we've been to the moon." Because by now, this also is old news. Well, then Linda's mother starts in on me. Please don't get me wrong, I love the old gal. But, frankly, if, God forbid, she died tomorrow, St. Peter would really have his hands full with the yak, yak, yak! So anyway, she says, "I didn't raise my daughter just so you could make smart remarks about her." And without thinking, I shoot back, "Well, I didn't buy that couch so an overweight relative could flatten the cushions out of shape by sitting on it all day." Well, I think you get the picture of how things are going at my house.

So anyway, Tuesday, I gotta fly to Detroit. Now God bless the airlines, they do a marvelous job, but come on, why are they always late? The last time I flew we were supposed to take off at 4:10 P.M. Now at 4:30 we still had not left the gate. I said to the stewardess, "Honey, what's the deal?" She shoots back kind of smart-alecky, "The pilot is waiting for some violent thunderstorm activity to clear the area." Violent thunderstorms? I say to myself, "She's a regular Willard Scott." So what can you do? Life is crazy and if I live to be 100 I'll never figure it out. Like those wackos in Washington. Or should I say, our distinguished Congress. I tell people, "You want to see a comedy show, put some cameras in Congress. Then you'll see some comedy." And now I see where these geniuses voted themselves a raise. Hey, didn't they just get a raise? But I'll tell you one thing in all seriousness. If that Berlin Wall hadn't come down, there could have been real trouble. So I think President Bush did a marvelous job on that one.

Let me just say one thing about Madonna and all her *Truth or Dare* stuff. *Truth or Dare*? The truth is, who cares? Have you seen this? Now they have these Madonna Wannabees. That's great! Just what we need!

I have the worst luck. The other day my wife and I are in the market and I pick out a can of soup. Just my luck, it's the only can of soup in the whole place that doesn't have a price on it. So what happens? The checkout kid gets on the P.A. and says, "Price check on a can of soup." Great! Now the whole market knows I'm buying soup. Just what I need. Well, like I said, that's the kind of luck I have. I don't think the kid meant any harm or anything. I don't think he even knew what he was doing really. When we got home, Linda and I had a pretty good laugh about it, but at the time, I'll be honest with you, I was steamed.

Do you have any stories like this? If you do, we'd love to read them. And, if we print one of your stories we'll send you fifty dollars. That's right, fifty dollars. Well, good luck and get going.

Dave Letterman

INTRODUCTION

Hello, Proud Bookowner!

And welcome to the wholesome and stimulating world of Top Ten Lists. We hope you and your family will enjoy this collection for years to come. We've designed it with your comfort and convenience in mind. No expense was spared in the sanitary, high-gloss cover materials or in the Space Age streamlined packaging which allows thousands of printed words to fit into a slim, rather unsubstantial book that folds easily, even when you don't want it to. And—despite warnings by the so-called "experts"—we've gone ahead and used paper for most of the pages. We think the results speak for themselves.

Now a word to those of you who are *not* Proud Bookowners. I'm addressing those of you who are standing and reading this volume in the bookstore, or have borrowed it from a gainfully employed friend or relative, or perhaps even sunk so low as to steal it from someone who *works* for a living and whose taxes will pay for *your* three-square-meals-a-day when you are inevitably captured and imprisoned. Listen to me, you cheap *punks*—you might think you're cute, but your kind makes me *sick*. I wish our Founding Fathers had not been so short-sighted when they extended basic human rights even to *filth* like you. I will not rest until the last of you blood-sucking parasites has been sent to eternal torment in your own special level of hell.

Once again, to our Proud Bookowners, my warmest personal regards!

—and "Welcome Aboard!"

Steve O'Donnell

Head Writer,
"Late Night with David Letterman"

TOP TEN MOST COMMON NEW YORK CITY HEALTH CODE VIOLATIONS

10. Hot dogs kept warm in street vendor's pants

9. Rat in rice canister not wearing a hairnet

8. Dishwasher replaced by St. Bernard who laps plates clean

7. Tank of live lobsters with wet hacking coughs

6. Kitchen full of shirtless fat guys soothing sunburns with raw veal

5. Fry cook not washing hands after strangling somebody

4. Raymond Burr's swimming trunks found in kettle of corn chowder

3. French onion soup thickened with Vaseline

2. Al Sharpton's hot tub

1. So-called "sidewalk pâté"

ORVILLE REDENBACHER'S TOP TEN MOST HORRIFYING SECRETS

10. That's not his grandson, that's his "longtime companion"

9. Has fifty pounds of plastic explosives taped to his body at all times

8. He was raised by white mice

7. Is the real voice of Milli Vanilli

6. Came home one night to find wife in bed with Keebler elves

5. Was responsible for that fire at the Jiffy Pop factory

4. Two words: Asian escorts

3. Has small vestigial wings

2. Likes to wear pants three sizes too large, go to malls, and then say "Oops!" whenever they fall down

1. That ain't butter

TOP TEN WAYS TO TELL YOU'RE POSSESSED

10. You feel stuffed even after a light dinner

9. Your voice sounds more and more like Bea Arthur's

8. You run around your Palm Beach house wearing nothing but an Oxford shirt

7. You ask the barber to cut your hair a little more like Hitler's

6. You find yourself wondering what sex with Cher would be like

5. You don't have to use rear-view mirror to look at the cars behind you

4. You're a former cast member of "Diff'rent Strokes"

3. Every time you hiccup, sparks fly out of your mouth

2. You become Vice President of the United States even though you are a total boob

1. When "Father Dowling" show comes on, your eyes start to sting

TOP TEN LEAST EFFECTIVE BITS OF INFIELD CHATTER

10. "Don't hit it here. I have trouble with grounders!"

9. "Hey, beer man! Two down here!"

8. "Your mother wears attractive pumps with a modest heel!"

7. "Hey, look! A barn swallow!"

6. "My name is Bill and I'm an alcoholic!"

5. "We're the Cleveland Indians!"

4. "Get this guy out—and I'll give you a big hug!"

3. "A hundred years from now, what difference will it make?"

2. "I'm really awfully sleepy!"

1. "Hey—it's only a game!"

TOP TEN TRICKS
YOU CAN PLAY ON
THE CENSUS TAKER

10. Excuse yourself from room and come back wearing different clothes. Repeat fifteen times.

9. Shout all your responses as if you were a contestant on "Family Feud"

8. Have two-headed friend hang out in living room. Ask if he counts as one person or two.

7. Repeatedly ask, "And how many Eskimos did we count today?"

6. Invite them to take a shower to freshen up—then keep flushing the toilet

5. Ask if you have to fill out form in pencil or if human blood is okay

4. Insist on First Amendment right to answer questions in mime

3. After his sixth beer, slip him a non-alcoholic one and see if he notices the difference

2. Two words: plastic vomit

1. Start going "168 million and *one* ... 168 million and *two*" so guy gets messed up and has to start counting all over again

TOP TEN FAST-FOOD FRANCHISES IN IRAQ

10. Kentucky Gassed Chicken

9. Sand-in-the-Box

8. Saddam's Big Boy

7. Goats 'n' Stuff

6. Veil-less Babes Donut Shop

5. Donkey Hut

4. Glorious Martyred Chicken Parts

3. Falafel Bell

2. Taco Tent

1. Stuff Your Hump

TOP TEN GROUNDS FOR JUSTIFIABLE HOMICIDE

10. Using CB lingo

9. Talking loudly in a restaurant about your bladder infection

8. Being a New Kid on the Block

7. Looking at someone wrong (New York City only)

6. Trying to start "the wave"

5. Repeatedly answering telephone "Yel-lo?"

4. Two words: vacation photos

3. Eating all the Cracklin' Oat Bran

2. Revealing the surprise ending to *Ernest Goes to Jail*

1. Constantly combing hair and asking passersby "Do you think I look like Jack Lord?"

TOP TEN NEW FEATURES ON *AIR FORCE ONE*

10. External P.A. system so President can greet drivers on interstate highways below

9. Coppertone banner for flying over beach

8. Bitchin' flame decals

7. Fake antenna to make people think they have a cellular phone on board

6. Button that transforms plane into glowing saucer to screw with farmers in Midwest

5. Plastic monster on wing to intimidate foreign dignitaries from Third World nations

4. Melon baller

3. Pet door for Millie—the President's flying dog

2. Stealth babes

1. Phony steering wheel so Vice President Quayle can pretend he's flying plane

TOP TEN THINGS THAT WILL GET YOU KICKED OUT OF THE MACY'S THANKSGIVING DAY PARADE

10. Every time float goes by, screaming at top of lungs, "She's gonna blow!"

9. Repeatedly asking total strangers if you can sit on their shoulders

8. Going up on Macy's roof; fishing for Willard's toupée

7. Throwing your hotel keys onto the float with Little Bo-Peep

6. Rubbing Kermit balloon on Al Sharpton's hair; then sticking it on the Chrysler Building

5. Cold-cocking Santa; taking his place dressed as Roy Orbison

4. Entering your own float: The Life-Size Beat-up Camaro with Fifteen Dudes Crammed in It

3. Taking a leak off to the side of the reviewing stand

2. Going on and on about how much better the Sears Thanksgiving Day parade is

1. Marching pantsless

TOP TEN WORK-RELATED INJURIES AT THE WHAM-O FACTORY

10. Pulled Slinky

9. Whiffle Welts

8. Decapitation by Experimental Razor Frisbee

7. Tripping Over Gummy Web of Silly String into Table Saw

6. Slip 'n' Slide 'n' Concussion

5. Overcome by Fumes from Batch of Custom-Order Toxic Play-Doh for Pentagon

4. Yo-yo Recoil Cranial Fracture

3. Burnt Tongue from Cafeteria Chili

2. Punctured Water Weenie

1. Hula-Hoop Chafing

TOP TEN DUTIES OF QUEEN ELIZABETH II

10. Gets to throw first punch at British soccer riots

9. Appear in TV ads for London Radio Shacks

8. Put on big furry hillbilly bear costume and greet visitors to Buckingham Palace

7. Feed the royal monkeys

6. Play local disc jockeys in donkey basketball games for charity

5. Represent the United Kingdom among the Gorgeous Ladies of Wrestling

4. Make Prince Andrew stop wearing T-shirt that says "Wanna see the royal jewels?"

3. Must chase, kill, and consume barn rats

2. Kick the queen of Sweden's ass in croquet

1. Tip like a big shot

TOP TEN REJECTED
NFL TEAM NAMES

10. The Opticians

9. The Groin-Pullers

8. The Fragile Porcelain Mice

7. The Fightin' Amish

6. The Blood-Swollen Ticks

5. The Velveteen Rabbits

4. The Referee Killers

3. The Soft Angora Sweater–Wearing Debutantes

2. The Greasy Ferrets

1. The Highly Paid Dumb Guys

TOP TEN PUNCH LINES
TO DIRTY JOKES
ASTRONAUTS TELL

10. You call *that* Mission Control?

9. The Titan Two, the Saturn Five, and Cher's water bed

8. Heat shields? I thought you said Brooke Shields!

7. Thirty seconds and holding—and please keep holding!

6. Hey! Blame gravity!

5. I said Venus! *Venus!*

4. Who do I look like? Buzz Aldrin?

3. 10, 9, 8, 7—oops!

2. It wasn't g-forces that killed that monkey

1. Gee—it *tasted* like Tang!

TOP TEN INEXPENSIVE WEEKEND ACTIVITIES IN NEW YORK CITY

10. Ruptured-pipe steam baths in middle of street

9. Take Bible out of hotel room drawer. Look out window. Circle the Commandments as you see them being broken.

8. Lie down in chalk body outlines to see if they fit

7. Rummage through meat plant dumpsters off 14th Street; try to assemble your own cow

6. Watch "America's Most Wanted," then go fugitive-spotting at the Port Authority

5. Using birdseed, get Columbus Circle pigeons to spell out nasty words

4. Try on pair of pants at Macy's, then walk around store asking everyone you see, "How do they look?"

3. Throw rocks at Chrysler Building and wait for Old Man Chrysler to come out and chase you away

2. Buy fake police ID in Times Square and strip-search self

1. Remember—the D in D Train is for *Dancing!*

TOP TEN GOVERNMENT EUPHEMISMS FOR A RECESSION

10. Lifestyle downscaling opportunity

9. Our Little Problem

8. The ugly, stupid cousin of robust growth

7. Something for you '30s nostalgia buffs

6. Cheap meat-eatin' days

5. A treat for our bankruptcy lawyer friends

4. A good time to switch to RC Cola

3. Still a hell of a lot better than any country in South America, pal

2. The National Bummer

1. It's Krazy Dollar Days!

TOP TEN AMISH SPRING BREAK ACTIVITIES

10. Drink molasses till you heave

9. Wet-bonnet contest

8. Stuff as many guys as you can into a buggy

7. Buttermilk kegger

6. Blow past the Dairy Queen on a really bitchin' Clydesdale

5. Get tattoo "Born to Raise Barns"

4. Cruise streets of Fort Lauderdale shouting insults at people with zippers

3. Sleep in until six A.M.

2. Drive over to Mennonite country and kick some ass

1. Churning butter naked

TOP TEN PET PEEVES OF GUYS WHO MANAGE BIG AND TALL MEN'S STORES

10. Fat guys who get their inseam measured a couple of times—and then don't buy anything

9. When a size fifty-four doesn't close the dressing room curtain all the way

8. When Roger Ebert tries to return old bathing suits

7. Annoying *thwack* sound when customer walks into ceiling fan

6. Never get to meet Jake, only get to meet the Fatman

5. When it's "Big and Tall Men's Store Managers Day" at the ballpark—and you have to work

4. When a big and tall guy gets wedged in a door frame and you have to call the fire department

3. Willard

2. While fitting a fat guy on your lunch hour, he asks if you're going to finish that sandwich

1. Broken chairs

TOP TEN BUSINESS AND BANKING TIPS FROM NEIL BUSH

10. Demand two pieces of ID before loaning a guy 100 million dollars

9. Business cards should include name, address, and phrase, "My dad's the President"

8. Read my lips: Cheat on taxes

7. Have old man call tactical nuclear strike on new bank across the street

6. Ask Quayle if he has two tens for a five. Repeat until you're rich.

5. When somebody pays you to repave their driveway, just use black paint

4. Slugs usually work in White House condom machine

3. Remind reporters that, unlike Ronald Reagan, Jr., you never wore leotards in your life

2. Big Gulp is best value at 7-Eleven

1. If accused of bank fraud, best defense is a simple and elegant "Oops!"

TOP TEN OTHER INVENTIONS BY THE SUICIDE MACHINE DOCTOR

10. The Craftmatic Adjustable Groin-Puller

9. The Mesh Parachute

8. Clorox Coladas

7. The Rickety Ladder

6. The Recipe for New Coke

5. The Steel-Bristle Retina Brush

4. The Frayed Asbestos Handkerchief

3. The Tub Toaster

2. The Denny's All-You-Can-Eat Seafood Special

1. The Popeil Pocket Suicide Machine

TOP TEN JOBS WITH MORE SECURITY THAN YANKEE MANAGER

10. Official car-starter for Mr. Gotti

9. Cleveland Indians World Series victory parade organizer

8. Colombian judge

7. Co-host on the "Today" show

6. Salesclerk in incredibly delicate porcelain vase shop, Beirut

5. Curator of the George Plimpton Museum in Harlem

4. Member of the New Monkees

3. Handyman who puts new nameplate on Yankee manager's door

2. Director of security at Dave Letterman's house

1. Guy who deflects things being thrown at Dan Quayle's head

TOP TEN SUMMER FUN TIPS FROM GENERAL ELECTRIC

10. Tie thousands of light bulbs together; raft down Colorado River

9. Huge electric turbines make great Frisbee launchers!

8. Put on softball mitts; try to catch defective G.E. jet engine parts as they drop from the sky

7. Fire someone

6. Try a zesty summer salad made from arugula and plenty of G.E. hundred-watt bulbs!

5. Kids love to play "Bury an Expensive American-Made VCR" at the beach

4. Install an air conditioner in your oven for food so cool it's hot!

3. Liven up meetings with Defense Department auditors with dozens of bikini-clad hookers!

2. Use your three-speed fan to make monster daiquiris!

1. Get a G.E. toaster tan!

TOP TEN LEAST POPULAR SUPERMARKET CHAINS

10. Pick 'n' Lick

9. Larva Town

8. Food Crypt

7. Risky's

6. Price Hiker

5. Rex Reed's Grocery Rodeo

4. The Expiration Date Grab Bag

3. I'm-Not-Wearing-Pantry

2. Hitler's

1. Bag This!

TOP TEN SIGNS THAT YOUR WIFE IS SEEING SINATRA

10. Without warning, she replaces the Paul Newman spaghetti sauce with the Frank Sinatra spaghetti sauce

9. She insists on doing all the grocery shopping in Las Vegas

8. Always leans on horn when she sees "Honk If You've Slept with Sinatra" bumper sticker

7. She starts praising the songwriting genius of Mr. Jimmy Van Heusen

6. Her rival in the PTA suddenly washes up in town reservoir

5. You turn on "Entertainment Tonight" and see Frank Sinatra wearing your pajamas

4. Always saying to your son, "Why can't you be more like that nice Frank Sinatra, Jr.?"

3. She's laughing just a little too hard at this list

2. People who owe her money for Tupperware suddenly begin paying up

1. She comes home smelling like a sweaty tuxedo

TOP TEN WAYS THE WORLD WOULD BE DIFFERENT IF EVERYONE WAS NAMED PHIL

10. Almost impossible to get personal license plate "Phil"

9. Ben and Jerry's ice cream now called Phil and Phil's

8. Expectant parents could be heard saying "Phil if it's a boy and Phil if it's a girl"

7. When caller to Donahue show said "Phil?" everyone in audience would reply "Yes?"

6. 007 fans look forward to classic line, "Bond. Phil Bond."

5. Instead of screaming, "Watch where you're going, you stupid bastard!" New Yorkers would scream, "Watch where you're going, Phil, you stupid bastard!"

4. Could throw an office into total confusion by calling and asking, "Is Tony there?"

3. Teenage pranksters would call airport and have them page Phil Hertz

2. Wouldn't have to look in *TV Guide* to see who's on the "The Tonight Show."

1. Most popular Beatle? Phil.

TOP TEN REJECTED
PROM THEMES

10. Let's Pretend We All Have Bright
    Futures

9. A Night at the Hair Club for Men

8. America's Most Wanted

7. Rise Up and Kill the Popular Kids

6. Children of the Damned

5. Sorry I Made You Pregnant

4. An Evening in Willie Nelson's Laundry Hamper

3. Come as Your Gay English Teacher

2. We Shall Not Pass This Way Again—
   Except for Our Really Depressing
   Reunion in About Ten Years

1. 'Faced!

TOP TEN
BIOENGINEERING
PROJECTS IN
DEVELOPMENT

10. Prairie dogs who change tires

9. Skunk that gives off lemon-fresh scent after being flattened by Mack truck

8. Sea otters who wear their fur like Pat Riley

7. Squids that wait for the cable guy

6. Super-intelligent dogs that really can play poker so you could just photograph them instead of buying one of those fancy novelty paintings

5. Popcorn kernels that pop—and then tell you the correct time and temperature

4. Cocoa Puffs bird with a calm, stable outlook on life

3. Angry, growling, hissing marigold

2. Mexican marital-counseling beans

1. A grinch who steals car radios

TOP TEN MARION BARRY CAMPAIGN SLOGANS

10. I'm addicted—to public service!

9. America's funniest home video

8. Just say yes

7. I'm a Kennedy

6. He's ready to personally confiscate drugs

5. Let's put a little Colombia into the District of Columbia

4. Hey—here's your Justice Department, pal!

3. He'll get the hookers off the streets— and into the hotel rooms

2. Imagine the victory party!

1. I'm Barry, Barry sorry

TOP TEN CATEGORIES ON IRAQI "JEOPARDY!"

10. Things that won't set off airport security alarms

9. Nicknames for sand

8. Famous Mohammeds

7. At home with Hitler

6. Games played with a human head

5. Ways to lose a hand

4. Twenty-three-letter words

3. Ayatollahs who have fallen out of their coffins

2. Sounds like "Shi'ite"

1. Broadway show tunes

TOP TEN GOOD THINGS
ABOUT NEW YORK

10. Can get car windows clean at every street corner

9. New rule: Autopsy results in less than a half hour—or it's free

8. Annual abandoned-auto show

7. Four words: Regis and Kathie Lee

6. Commotion during mob hits at steakhouses allows you to skip out on check

5. The Japanese keep their buildings looking nice

4. Plenty of empty seats in Manhattan churches

3. 911 is a toll-free call

2. The best-looking hookers in the world!

1. The sickening filth, deafening noise, and terrifying danger offset by a $3 cup of coffee

TOP TEN UMPIRE COMPLAINTS

10. Having to carpool with team mascot

9. Line-up card from Don Zimmer always smeared with spaghetti sauce

8. When a manager who's yelling right in your face suddenly kisses you

7. Have to use glass-bottom shower over concession stand

6. When they show your wife in bed with some other guy on Diamondvision

5. Players who ask if you would scratch them

4. All those empty Slim-Fast containers around Dodger dugout

3. When the San Diego chicken steals your street clothes and sets them on fire during his pregame dance

2. In most states, "killing the umpire" only a class B misdemeanor

1. Squat burns

TOP TEN PERKS TO BEING ONE OF *US* MAGAZINE'S TEN MOST BEAUTIFUL WOMEN

10. Free coffee with fill-up at participating Texaco

9. Fewer hassles when applying for a commercial fishing license

8. Become subject of late-night discussions in prison

7. Stunning bone structure creates a good diversion when shoplifting

6. Power to dispatch U.S. troops anywhere in the hemisphere without consulting Congress

5. Less time waiting around in supermarkets because you can now use the "World's Ten Most Beautiful Women" checkout aisle

4. Get to cruelly speculate as to who was number eleven

3. Lifetime membership in Kraft Macaroni & Cheese Club

2. Your picture in the back rooms of muffler shops everywhere

1. Counterboy at McDonald's usually tosses in a couple extra ketchups without you having to ask

TOP TEN SIGNS SUMMER'S OVER IN HELL

10. Ayatollah no longer walks around with zinc oxide on his nose

9. Molten lava slide closes for season

8. Only television station switches from round-the-clock reruns of "Who's the Boss?" to *all-new* episodes of "Who's the Boss?"

7. Anguished cries for ice water replaced by anguished cries for cider and doughnuts

6. Satan begins annual fretting about whether it would be cheaper to switch the whole system over to natural gas

5. Tours less crowded to see future home of Saddam Hussein

4. Hell's weatherman starts to make jokes about "freezing over"

3. Giant groundhog comes out of his hole, sees his shadow, and eats five people

2. Season begins for hell's official football team—the New York Jets

1. Sign-up sheets posted for hayrides with Hitler

TOP TEN ELF OCCUPATIONAL HAZARDS

10. Severe chafing from testing new bicycle seats

9. Tinsel lung

8. Mistakenly drinking paint

7. Jingle bell lodged in trachea

6. A reindeer taking a leak on you

5. Stepping on a little red wagon and sliding into giant gas turbines

4. Ringworm

3. Lawn darts

2. Fired when G.E. takes over company

1. Hammer fights

TOP TEN FREAK ACCIDENTS ON THE "TODAY" SHOW SET

10. Tour group mauled after teasing Willard during feeding time

9. Makeup artist scratches arm on Faith Daniels' hair

8. High-powered floor waxer runs wild; kills a guy

7. Gene Shalit electrocuted by frayed microphone cord; decides to leave his hair that way

6. Meteor plunges into Bryant's coffee cup; splashes guest George Will

5. A series of suspicious toupée fires

4. Unwrapping of forgotten Jane Pauley tuna sandwich knocks out several staffers

3. Willard attacked by rabid duck at one of those state fairs or wherever the hell it is he goes

2. Guest on Donahue's "homicidal pyro-maniacs" segment wanders into wrong studio

1. Glare from Joe Garagiola's head blinds boom operator

GEORGE BUSH'S TOP TEN STRESS BUSTERS

10. Menthol rubdowns from Sununu

9. Calls Mike Dukakis; asks if "Lou Zer" is there

8. Makes Secret Service agents ride bicycles into White House pool; tapes it for "America's Funniest Home Videos"

7. Two words: malt liquor

6. Takes off pants; sits on picture of Dan Rather

5. Picks up hitchhikers on the Beltway; tells them about his grandchildren

4. Gives First Lady the "ol' presidential pardon," if you know what I mean

3. Relaxes with Marion Barry

2. Tosses horseshoes at Quayle's head

1. Has Barbara tell him again and again how he's overcome the wimp factor

TOP TEN LEAST POPULAR
NEW CAR OPTIONS

10. Rear window fogger

9. Pre-filled ashtrays

8. Passenger airbag in trunk

7. Drifter in the back seat who says "Your door is open"

6. Hydraulic roadkill scoop

5. Thirty-five smelly Ringling Brothers clowns

4. Ceiling fans

3. Electronic scanner that reads the mind of Roddy McDowell

2. Oprahometer

1. Intermittent steering

TOP TEN WAYS NBC NEWS CAN SAVE MONEY

10. Make stuff up

9. Somehow incorporate news items into "The Cosby Show"

8. Sneak in plugs like "The shuttle's reentry was as smooth as an ice-cold Budweiser"

7. Stop buying G.E. bulbs and get some that don't burn out so fast

6. Arthur Kent kissing booth

5. Generic fruit punch

4. Limit news coverage to things that happen in the building

3. Fire Dr. Art Ulene (Whoops! They already did that!)

2. Water down the ketchup

1. Every night have Brokaw turn on portable TV and say "Shall we watch the CBS news together?"

TOP TEN MOST FREQUENTLY RETURNED CHRISTMAS GIFTS

10. The Sunbeam Six-Slice Shower Toaster

9. Raymond Burr's "Sweatin' to the Oldies" videocassette

8. New York Jets playoff tickets

7. *The Devout Muslim Nation Joke Book*

6. The Black and Decker Forehead Sander

5. Bag of live mice

4. Super-Itchy Slipper-Socks from Super-Itchy Technologies, Hartford, Connecticut

3. Dr. Kevorkian's Suicide Machine

2. Hickory Farms Cologne

1. "Lick Me"—The Board Game

SADDAM HUSSEIN'S TOP TEN HELPFUL INVASION TIPS

10. *Don't* phone ahead

9. Start with something easy—like France

8. Make sure everybody uses the rest room *before* your armored columns rumble across international borders

7. Don't feed the raccoons at KOA campsites

6. Nerve gas: Don't leave home without it

5. If "Nightline" calls for an interview, make sure Ted Koppel's doing show, not Forrest Sawyer

4. Take along a gift for your host—for example, a puppet regime

3. Point out that people *liked* the British invasion of the '60s

2. Plenty of change for tollbooths

1. Don't just race through a country, take some time to stop and smell the goats

MILLIE'S TOP TEN PET PEEVES

10. Never any table scraps under Barbara's chair

9. Getting the blame every time Marlin Fitzwater takes a leak on the couch

8. When Quayle hogs the dog toys

7. Spuds Mackenzie

6. When the Korean ambassador gets hungry

5. Barney Frank's flaming poodle

4. Having same name as that idiot "Vanilli"

3. When Marion Barry bogarts your last joint

2. Being known as "the First Bitch"

1. When Reagan shows up in his pajamas murmuring, "Nice kitty, nice kitty"

TOP TEN REASONS
NEW YORK CITY WOULD
BE A GOOD PLACE
FOR THE OLYMPICS

10. No shortage of starter pistols

9. Already have cute mascot—Lou the Giant Rat

8. New York Yankees set the tone for amateur athletics

7. Eternal flame ceremony enhanced by mile-long parade of arsonists

6. Would give city's cab drivers chance to cheer for their home countries in person

5. Exciting new exhibition sport: turnstile jumping

4. Extra traffic easily handled by city's clean and efficient monorail system

3. Plenty of room for out-of-town visitors at Letterman's place

2. Fun for Olympians to compare neck burns where gold medals used to be

1. Hudson River practically made for synchronized swimming

TOP TEN MR. WIZARD EXPERIMENTS

10. Let's flush a canned ham down the toilet

9. Will your head fit here?

8. What happens when you lick a wasp's nest?

7. Getting free HBO

6. How many beers before you make a pass at Bea Arthur?

5. How much Crisco can you eat?

4. Substituting Folgers Crystals for freshly brewed coffee

3. Dressing like *Mrs.* Wizard

2. Big pockets for super shoplifting

1. Those two flight attendants in Dallas

TOP TEN SIGNS THAT TRUMP IS IN TROUBLE

10. Had the cable company disconnect Cinemax

9. Trump Shuttle now used to haul lumber

8. Attracting a lower class of bimbo

7. Recently asked advisors how they thought a "battling billionaire" character would go over on the pro-wrestling circuit

6. Has been sucking up to Merv

5. This morning, he had himself evicted

4. In 7-Eleven, was heard saying "I'm really thirsty" and yet suspiciously did *not* order a Big Gulp

3. Now does tacky, embarrassing things on a much smaller scale

2. Just got a paper route

1. He takes Dave Letterman's calls

TOP TEN GOOD THINGS ABOUT BEING A REALLY, REALLY DUMB GUY

10. Never have to sit through long, boring Nobel Prize banquet

9. Pleasant sense of relief when Road-runner gets away from Coyote

8. G.E. executive dining room has great clam chowder

7. Seldom interrupted by annoying request to "Put that in layman's terms"

6. Get to have own talk show with Canadian bandleader

5. Stallone might play you in the movie

4. Can feel superior to really, really, *really* dumb guys

3. May get to be Vice President of the United States

2. Already know the answer when people ask, "What are you—an idiot?"

1. Fun bumper sticker: I'd Rather Be Drooling

TOP TEN SLOGANS FOR THE NEW McLEAN BURGER

10. Now it takes twice as long to clog your arteries

9. Not only secret sauce—secret meat!

8. Developed after Mayor McCheese's double bypass

7. Almost as tasty as those green shakes we sell around St. Patrick's Day

6. Okay, the McNuggets suck. But these are good! Really!

5. Why not spend the day chewing?

4. Consult your physician if dizziness occurs

3. Eat me

2. If this was around in 1965, Elvis would be alive today

1. Give it a try, fat boy

TOP TEN LEAST POPULAR SUMMER CAMPS

10. Camp Tick in beautiful Lyme, Connecticut

9. Camp Geraldo

8. Backyards-of-People-Who Don't-Seem-to-Be-Home Tenting Holidays

7. Amish Computer Camp

6. Dr. Kevorkian's Build-Your-Own-Suicide-Machine and Tennis Camp

5. Mr. and Mrs. Johnson's Camp for Kids Whose Parents Don't Love Them, Don't Want Them Around, and Won't Even Pay for a Halfway Decent Camp

4. Gerry Cooney's Camp for Big Clumsy White Kids

3. Incontinent Palomino Western Trail Ranch

2. Camp Sissy-Boy

1. Mickey Rooney's All-Nude Outward Bound

TOP TEN IRAQI NICKNAMES FOR GEORGE BUSH

10. Sherry-swilling yacht-monkey

9. Satan's lambada partner

8. Quayle picker

7. Four-Eyes

6. The-never-had-anyone-even-close-to-Marilyn-Monroe President

5. Pork-rind-munching goofball

4. Yale-educated father of five (Okay, they're not all so bad.)

3. Nancy Reagan's dress dummy

2. Trust fund weenie

1. Mr. Scared-of-Broccoli

TOP TEN THINGS WITH THE SAME STATISTICAL PROBABILITY AS THE MINNESOTA TWINS TURNING TWO TRIPLE PLAYS

10. First ball of season hurled by President actually reaches catcher without bouncing

9. Falling meteor crushes Ebert, spares Siskel

8. No one within two miles wearing a Simpsons T-shirt

7. Farrakhan named B'nai B'rith Man of the Year

6. A really, really dumb guy becomes Vice President

5. That Jason guy once again coming back from the dead again to terrorize unsuspecting coeds camping by the lake

4. Watching VH-1 for a half hour and not seeing a Phil Collins video

3. Watching VH-1 for a half hour

2. President Tyson

1. The Yankees making one double play

TOP TEN REJECTED CRAYOLA COLORS

10. Bruise Purple

9. Bus Station Brown

8. Exxon Spill Gray

7. Shecky Green

6. Scorched Flesh

5. Off Whitey

4. You're Just Plain Yellow

3. Ochre Winfrey

2. Jaundice

1. Cholesterol Beige

TOP TEN REASONS
EASTERN AIRLINES
WENT BANKRUPT

10. Lavish keep-the-whole-can-of-soda policy

9. Free solid-gold headphones in coach

8. Spent small fortune at crew lounges sending complimentary cocktails to Northwest pilots

7. Shouldn't have copied Domino's Pizza campaign: "If you're not there in 30 minutes—the flight's free!"

6. Insane policy of hiring dozens of M.I.T. physicists just to make sure the dessert squares were perfectly square

5. You think it doesn't cost money to falsify safety records?

4. Could've saved money on jumbo economy-sized containers of jet fuel instead of impulsively buying little cans of it at corner convenience store

3. Huge wallet where they kept their money stolen during recent trip to New York

2. Baggage handler Walter F. Collins of 1411 Hillturn Lane, Cincinnati, Ohio, who, *damn it*, just didn't hustle

1. You try giving away free bags of peanuts year after year after year!

TOP TEN APRIL FOOL'S DAY JOKES IN NEW YORK CITY

10. Super Glue an automatic weapon to curb and watch passersby try to pick it up

9. Put fake vomit on sidewalk right next to real vomit

8. Suicide hotline puts you on hold while playing Van Halen's "Jump"

7. Hold Wisconsin couple at gunpoint; demand their money and jewelry— then give them back their jewelry

6. Adding a tail to chalk body outlines

5. Screaming, "The stock market is down!" then tossing life-sized dummy off roof of building

4. Instead of Miranda warning, cops say "You have the right to commit crimes"

3. Putting a "kick me" sign on guy's back before you throw him in East River

2. Cab drivers speak perfect English

1. Crack dens replace regular crack that is usually smoked there with Folgers Crystals

TOP TEN REJECTED BOWL GAME TITLES

10. The Ben-Gay Bowl

9. The White Guys All-Star Game

8. The Cupless Classic

7. The Festival of Big Sweaty Men on Steroids

6. I-Don't-Think-It's-a-Fracture-But-I-Can't-Be-Sure-Until-We-Take-Some-X-Rays Bowl

5. Our Dark Lord Satan's

4. The Guys-Who-Came-Really-Close-to-Passing-Their-Drug-Test Classic

3. Tournament of Hoses

2. Sissy-Boy Slap Party

1. Manute Bowl

TOP TEN DOG EXCUSES FOR LOSING THE DOG SHOW

10. Mistaken in assumption there would be chance to show off talent for drinking from toilet

9. Thought I saw that little chuckwagon

8. Bad idea going to Don King's barber

7. Caught in a lie claiming to be Cycle Two dog when I'm really Cycle Three

6. Shouldn't have picked Quayle as running mate

5. My lifelong battle with problem drool

4. During spelling portion, spelled "ubiquitous" with two B's

3. Didn't know that was the judge's leg

2. Money goes to trainer anyway, so let *him* stand naked in Madison Square Garden and get touched by a stranger in a bad suit

1. Like me, the whole thing was fixed

TOP TEN ATTRACTIONS AND EXHIBITS AT THE NIXON LIBRARY

10. G. Gordon Liddy kissing booth

9. Bust of Spiro Agnew made of Karamel Korn

8. Gag pardon signed by Professor Irwin Corey

7. Carny game: Guess the deleted expletive and win a stuffed toy

6. Pant leg where Chinese pandas had a little accident

5. Gerald Ford backyard stunt show

4. Five o'clock shadow petting zoo

3. Julie and Tricia petting zoo

2. "At least I wasn't Quayle" T-shirts

1. Ride the Tricky Dick—the tallest roller coaster west of the Rockies!

AL SHARPTON'S TOP TEN TRAVEL TIPS

10. To avoid overweight charges for your luggage, wear as many of your medallions as possible

9. Don't forget the electrical adapter for your blow dryer

8. All foreign food is good if you bring your own gravy

7. Before making reservations, make sure hotel has fat-guy suite

6. If hair pomade is not available in Far East, duck sauce will work

5. March on Buckingham Palace to protest the fact that there hasn't been a black king in years

4. When in Venice, have them load up front end of gondola with sacks of peat moss to balance you out in the back

3. If the Pope tries wearing some big medallion, go ahead and wear *two*

2. Be careful: in some countries, being loud and obnoxious is considered rude

1. Trust me: one jogging suit is all you'll need

TOP TEN POST-MISSION MAINTENANCE CHORES ON THE SPACE SHUTTLE

10. Return seats to upright position

9. Vacuum up Tang that spilled on carpet

8. Reset coordinates on death ray so people don't know we had it pointed at Rex Reed's house

7. Throw away old ketchup packets in glove compartment

6. Take shuttle to street corner in Lower Manhattan to get windshield squeegeed

5. Get roadies to unload amps and drum kit

4. Hose down the area where they had zero-gravity pie-eating contest

3. Scrape off strange pulsing podlike thing that attached itself to wing. Toss in trash. Forget about it.

2. Pull twin beds apart

1. Fill up tank and record mileage. Please leave keys in shuttle.

TOP TEN LEAST EXCITING SUPERPOWERS FOR COMIC BOOK SUPERHEROES

10. Super spelling

9. Lightning-fast mood swings

8. Really bendy thumb

7. Unusually natural smile when posing for photographs

6. Ability to calm jittery squirrels

5. Power to shake exactly two aspirin out of a bottle

4. Ability to get tickets to Goodwill Games

3. Power to score with other super-heroes' wives

2. Ability to communicate with corn

1. Magnetic colon

TOP TEN WAYS DAN QUAYLE CAN BUILD UP PUBLIC CONFIDENCE

10. Borrow those fake glasses Stallone wears to look smarter

9. Have his dad give everybody five bucks

8. Think of snappy comeback to that "You're no John F. Kennedy" zinger

7. Lip-synch all speeches to prerecorded voice of James Earl Jones

6. Go on "American Gladiators" and kick ass in the atlasphere

5. Do that trick where it looks like you're pulling off part of your thumb but you're really just moving other thumb

4. Appear before Senate subcommittee on multiplication tables

3. Announce with quiet determination that he's leaving politics

2. Get Bush to stop wearing "I'm with Stupid" T-shirt

1. Win "Vice-Presidents Week" on "Jeopardy!"

TOP TEN SURPRISES IN THE MR. PEANUT AUTOBIOGRAPHY

10. First name: Keith

9. His mother was half cashew

8. Sleeps in a big pile of dirt

7. Divorced first Mrs. Peanut after she became involved with a bag of trail mix

6. The Pillsbury Doughboy? Gay as a tangerine.

5. Peanut language not that different from English

4. Once shot out TV screen when Robert Goulet appeared on it

3. Belongs to a country club that doesn't admit pistachios

2. High school guidance counselor told him he'd never be anything but a huge unemployed freak

1. Once arrested wandering New York's Port Authority at dawn chanting, "Eat me!"

TOP TEN FEATURES OF SADDAM HUSSEIN'S BUNKER

10. Goat-sized microwave

9. State-of-the-art mustache-grooming facilities

8. A Gideon Koran

7. Button to launch Scud missiles hooked up to a Clapper

6. Security camera to catch woman who keeps breaking into bunker claiming to be Mrs. Hussein

5. Cheesy-looking clock that was gift from the PLO that he has to pull out every time Arafat visits

4. Babe-o-Matic Periscope

3. Wax museum featuring legends of the Old West

2. Shower (never used)

1. Hitler's old La-Z-Boy recliner

TOP TEN OTHER NICKNAMES FOR ABRAHAM LINCOLN

10. The Abe-o-litionist

9. Vanilla Abe

8. Town Car

7. Old Five-Dollar-Bill Boy

6. Grand Champion, Four Years Running, White House Slam Dunk Contest

5. Mr. Television, If It Had Been Invented

4. Mary Todd's Old Man (hippies only)

3. The Linckster

2. The Illinois Babe Magnet

1. Aaaaaaaaaaaabe

TOP TEN SIGNS YOU'RE IN LOVE WITH SECRETARY OF TRANSPORTATION SAMUEL K. SKINNER

10. You read nine newspapers a day in hopes of seeing his name

9. You believe his speeches are filled with secret messages to you

8. You hate the other cabinet members for holding him back

7. In your new wallet, where it says "In case of emergency, please notify," you've filled in "Samuel K. Skinner"

6. You don't mind that he's just a secretary

5. You've put posters of him up right over your old posters of former Transportation Secretary James Burnley

4. Your two cats are named Samuel and Skinner

3. You keep breaking into his house claiming to be Mrs. Skinner

2. You drive fifty-five, hoping he'll notice

1. You come to after being hit with a two-by-four and say, "Forget about me. How's Samuel K. Skinner?"

SOME GUY NAMED JIM'S TOP TEN NAMES FOR HIS NEW HAT STORE

10. Jimbo's Cap Shack

9. Jim's Brims

8. Admiral Jim's Hats Ahoy!

7. The Jim O'Shantery

6. Hats 'Я' Jim

5. Jim's Bulletproof/Knifeproof/Spitproof Hats (New York City only)

4. Jim, Your Hat Smells Terrific!

3. Wally's Hat Stop (under new management)

2. If You Don't Want a Hat, Then Screw You

1. Colonel Jim's Kentucky Fried Hats

TOP TEN GOOD THINGS
ABOUT TED KENNEDY

10. Not the kind of person who snobbishly insists on wearing pants

9. Holds high score on Pac-Man machine at Au Bar

8. Does hilarious imitation of that Pepperidge Farm guy

7. Cried when Gary character died on "thirtysomething"

6. Ate his own weight in McRibs before limited time offer expired

5. Doesn't hog the NordicTrack

4. Will never become an embarrassing U.S. President

3. Does a great job as San Diego chicken

2. Proof that you can become a U.S. senator even though your family has hundreds of millions of dollars

1. Every time he gets away with something, it drives Nixon nuts

TOP TEN PROMOTIONAL SLOGANS FOR THE SUICIDE MACHINE

10. Just try it once—that's all we ask

9. The quicker putter-downer

8. Isn't it about time you took an honest look at your stinking, miserable life?

7. From the people who brought you The Clapper

6. Impress the chicks in hell

5. Claus Von Bulow says, "I liked it so much, I bought the company!"

4. While I'm killing myself, I'm also cleaning my oven

3. Dammit! It's time you did something for *you!*

2. If you're not dead in thirty minutes— it's free!

1. We're *not* the Heartbeat of America

TOP TEN REJECTED GIMMICKS FOR DOUBLEMINT GUM

10. The Doublemint Drifter

9. The Double-Bypass Twins

8. The Doublemint Pack of Vicious Dogs that Knock Over Garbage Cans and Bite Kids

7. The One Dentist out of Five Who Doesn't Recommend Trident

6. The Doublemint Bachelor and His Longtime Companion

5. MacNeil and Lehrer: Those Gum-Loving Newshounds

4. The Doublemint Woman with Multiple Personalities

3. Charles Manson in Swimming Trunks

2. The Doublemint Triplets with Bob Guccione in a Hot Tub

1. Hitler 'n' Hussein: the Mint Boys

TOP TEN IRAQI THANKSGIVING TRADITIONS

10. Loudly giving thanks for Saddam Hussein just in case the house is bugged

9. Turkey carved by oldest family member who still has hands

8. Watching the Baghdad Bengals beat the Jets

7. Stuffing the turkey—with plastic explosives

6. Go to Adrian's mom's house and hang out (I'm sorry. That's a *Rocky* Thanksgiving tradition.)

5. Eat huge pile of sand; doze off in front of TV

4. Watch Macy's parade via satellite; renew vow to kill Willard Scott

3. Slow-cook turkey with poison gas

2. Put on red foam clown noses; squirt each other with seltzer (I'm sorry. That's a *wacky* Thanksgiving tradition.)

1. Have nice dinner; then take over small defenseless country

TOP TEN WAYS THE CIVIL WAR SERIES WOULD BE DIFFERENT IF IT WERE ON NBC

10. General Grant played by Alf

9. Reenactment of Gettysburg featuring bottles of Bud *vs.* bottles of Bud Light

8. Diary excerpts punched up to include more "zingers"

7. Stonewall Jackson leads troops into battle at the wheel of a cool talking car

6. Early in war Lincoln replaces General McClellan with Deborah Norville

5. As cannonballs rain down on Fort Sumter, Bob Costas comments, "That's gotta hurt!"

4. More emphasis on Mathew Brady's photographs of swimsuit models

3. Willard Scott cameo as Clara Barton

2. Lincoln shot while watching taping of "The Golden Girls"

1. Would have pit Fanelli brother against Fanelli brother

TOP TEN CHANGES IN MOUNT RUSHMORE

10. Time and temperature display in Theodore Roosevelt's forehead

9. Removed big earrings from Lincoln because they made him look cheap

8. Add Morey Amsterdam

7. Elegant new Washington's Nose Café

6. Roosevelt and Jefferson now kissing

5. Loud, untidy family of squatters evicted from Lincoln's ear

4. Gag space that says "Reserved for Dan Quayle"

3. Giant mechanical hand added that slaps them across face like the Three Stooges

2. Genuine sheepskin eyebrows

1. The whole thing will be crawling with real live monkeys

TOP TEN PETE ROSE
PRISON ACTIVITIES

10. Making thousands of "FAY SUX" license plates

9. Trying to keep cellmate from getting to first base

8. Practicing opening and closing cell door to prepare for future as professional casino greeter

7. Playing Tevye in the all–tax evader version of *Fiddler on the Roof*

6. Executing his famous head-first slide over and over until he burrows highway to freedom

5. Discussing George Will's fascinating baseball book with members of Manson family

4. Starting "the wave" during prison riots

3. Getting a cell ready for Steinbrenner

2. Leading a seminar in scratching yourself

1. During softball game in exercise yard, arguing with umpire, getting thrown out of prison

TOP TEN SIGNS SCHOOL IS OUT IN NEW YORK CITY

10. Metal detectors freed up for use at public pools

9. East River barge traffic unimpeded by floating truant officers

8. Impossible to get tickets for big Monet retrospective

7. Powdered mashed potato wholesaler goes on vacation

6. Afternoon show at Strip World now filled with shop teachers

5. Movie theater matinees are less crowded

4. Extra-long lines to rob Good Humor man

3. The libraries are filled with conscientious young people keeping up with their studies (Sorry, that's a sign school is out in *Japan*.)

2. Lots of alarms going off

1. Teachers' wounds beginning to heal up

TOP TEN COURSES TAKEN BY BASKETBALL PLAYERS AT UNLV

10. Investing Your Illegal Recruiting Money Wisely

9. NBA Team Mascots: Are They Really Big Animals?

8. Naming the Presidents Since Kennedy

7. Hydraulic Principles of the Keg

6. Your Ass from a Hole in the Ground: A Comparative Study

5. The College Classroom: A Simulation

4. Nudie Paintings from the Olden Days

3. Copying Off the Exam of the Asian Guy in Front of You

2. How to Spell Tarkanian

1. How to Choose the Best Free Car

TOP TEN LEAST POPULAR MTV CONTESTS

10. Win Stuff Found in ZZ Top's Beards

9. Do Time for James Brown

8. Locked-in-Sting's-Car-Trunk Fantasy Weekend

7. A Date with Cher (must be under 16 years of age)

6. Win Michael Jackson's Old Nose

5. Actually Get to Be One of the New Monkees—Not for a Day, but Forever

4. 100th Caller Gets to Have Dinner with 101st Caller

3. Shirt Shopping with Paul Shaffer

2. Peter, Paul, and *You!*

1. Try on Meat Loaf's Pants

TOP TEN NEW SOURCES OF ENERGY

10. Harness static cling in Joe Garagiola's pants

9. Build hydroelectric dam to utilize flow of spit on New York City streets

8. In cold and flu season, use foreheads of feverish youngsters to warm dinner rolls

7. Jackie Onassis thought to be hoarding vast reserves of soft coal in her East Side apartment

6. Put Curly on a treadmill; stuff beehive in his pants

5. Make use of steam that comes out of Quayle's ears when he tries to do long division

4. Big friendly birds

3. Tap megadose of radiation given off by TV's broadcasting "Late Night" program

2. How about Superman getting off his ass?

1. Harness the sexual tension between MacNeil and Lehrer

PEOPLE'S TOP TEN EXCUSES FOR NOT FILLING OUT THE CENSUS

10. They're shy

9. For some reason, thought it was an order form for sea monkeys

8. You can't even win anything

7. Waiting until after operation so I can list self as "woman"

6. Thought going to the window and yelling "Here!" was good enough

5. Wasn't sure if, like on "Jeopardy!" answers had to be in form of question

4. Didn't know whether to count hostages in basement as boarders

3. Hoping one of the census babes will come to my house in person

2. Waiting for help with the big words from wife, Marilyn Quayle

1. Hey! I took part in "Hands Across America"—you should've just counted us then

TOP TEN REASONS TO GIVE DAN QUAYLE A RAISE

10. To begin teaching him the value of money

9. He has to replace the crayons he ate

8. His father threatened to make trouble

7. To match the salary of Millie, the White House dog

6. You'd rather he went out and got a real job and maybe screwed up an entire industry?

5. So he'll stop selling his autograph at *Star Trek* conventions

4. To show appreciation for his defending Indiana during the Vietnam War

3. To keep the money out of the hands of undeserving teachers and firefighters

2. Oh, what the hell—they're only giving him play money anyway

1. The White House lawn has been looking pretty darn sharp lately

TOP TEN TOP SECRET PROJECTS AT BIRDSEYE VILLAGE

10. A strain of lima beans with a refreshing menthol center

9. A way to send hollandaise sauce over a fax machine

8. Spinach that actually makes you really strong for a couple of minutes

7. Defrosting Walt Disney

6. TV show with a fat guy and a skinny guy who review movies and plug frozen vegetables

5. Test-marketing actual frozen birds' eyes

4. Sexy Swedish twins (not a product, just something for the boys in the lab)

3. Scud missile that seeks out and destroys the old guy in the Pepperidge Farm ad

2. A new less-embarrassing name for Niblets

1. Nerve peas

TOP TEN PERKS OF BEING SADDAM HUSSEIN, JR.

10. Can use poison gas on paper route customers who don't tip

9. Can cash check without ID at Baghdad Winn-Dixie

8. On your birthday can have Abu Nidal dressed in clown costume drive truck bomb into cake

7. Though completely unqualified, can get high-paying job with Iraqi Savings and Loan Company

6. Those madman-to-madman chats with Dad

5. Can take a leak in the fountain at the mall

4. CIA gives you candy bars in exchange for papers from Dad's briefcase

3. Get to play with latest biological weapons before the whole army has them

2. One phone call from Dad gets you a safe, cushy position with the National Guard

1. When you turn twenty-one, you get your own bunker

TOP TEN MAFIA EUPHEMISMS FOR DEATH

10. Checked into the Wooden Waldorf

9. No longer eligible for the census

8. Dropping both AT&T and MCI

7. Your highway taxes at work

6. Playing harp duets with Hoffa

5. Went into the mannequin business

4. Resting his organs

3. He's a roadie in Rock 'n' Roll Heaven

2. Kicked the oxygen habit

1. Bought a Yugo

TOP TEN WAYS TO GET OUT OF JURY DUTY

10. Bring note from Rusty the Bailiff

9. Ask if you get to execute criminals personally

8. Keep saying very loudly, "Hey, who's frying baloney?"

7. Every five minutes point to different person in courtroom and yell, "He did it!"

6. Say you're looking forward to hearing judge sing—like on "Cop Rock"

5. Ask if there will be opportunities to examine bloody undershirts

4. Fly into a rage whenever Norwegians are mentioned

3. Respond to every question with "Let me talk to the little man who lives in my pants"

2. Tell them you've already done jury duty on "Matlock"

1. Ask the judge if he's wearing Aramis

TOP TEN LEAST POPULAR PAY-PER-VIEW SPECIALS

10. All-American Rasping Cough-off

9. Magician Doug Henning Gets His Teeth Cleaned

8. An Evening with a Guy Who Kind of Looks Like Frank Sinatra

7. White NBA Players' All-Star Game

6. Raymond Burr's Night of a Hundred Pants

5. Texas Rangers Batting Practice

4. Live from the Arctic Circle—It's a Big Melting Iceberg!

3. Whittle-Mania!

2. The Time-to-Make-the-Doughnuts Guy: Up Close and Personal

1. The Liver Capades

TOP TEN THINGS SCHWARZKOPF HAS TO DO TO GET A FIFTH STAR

10. Sell more cookies than anyone else in his unit

9. During his next "20/20" interview, punch Hugh Downs

8. Every time he calls President Bush have friend make machine-gun and bomb noises in background so it'll seem like he's still fighting really hard

7. Hope that somehow Pizza Hut has a promotion: "Eat five pizzas—get a fifth U.S. general star free!"

6. Capture LAPD Chief Daryl Gates

5. Beat Sergeant Slaughter in best two out of three falls in "Wrestlemania"

4. Somehow fix it so White House gets free HBO

3. Hope and pray that Bob Guccione doesn't print the nude photos

2. Do at least a halfway decent job on the parallel parking

1. Do some five-star butt-kissing

Clifford T. Bell, about three months old.

The shed outside Portland in which Bell was born on Armistice Day. The porch was later destroyed in the accident with the paper boy. *(AP/Wide World Photos)*

Bell's parents, James Huntington Bell ("The Colonel") and Florence Dunbar Bell, outside The Conservatory shortly before their dismissal. *(AP/Wide World Photos)*

One of the Bell family "hoop-dee-doos" (as The Colonel called them) on Elmwood Avenue. The photographer was probably Clifford himself.

Young Clifford, still at Forestry School, with one of the many plaques he purchased secondhand. He had already drawn up crude plans for what would become the Bell Water Drill.

Some of the tires confiscated during the July Fourth raid. *(United Press International photo)*

The war barely over, construction began on Bell's casino in Las Vegas. It was one of the first on The Strip. *(Las Vegas News Bureau)*

Returning servicemen loved *The Musical Canteen.* Bell provided the voice for the popular Furry Francis.

The fanatically devoted team of bodyguards that the press would briefly call "The Memphis Mafia." Bell insisted on the embroidered names and the neckties.

Professional bowler Dick Weber in a lighter moment, before the bitter parting of ways with Bell over the wording of the brochure. *(United Press International photo)*

The scene outside the Kansas City "fund-raiser." *(AP/Wide World Photos)*

President Harry S. Truman increasingly distanced himself from Bell and denied sending the box of pears which Bell repeatedly showed to reporters. *(AP/Wide World Photos)*

To improve his image, Bell funded this Teen Center in Santiago, Chile, even though he had never visited the city and knew next to nothing about it. *(United Press International photo)*

Official photographs released by the Houston Police Department following the trouble at the parade. The serial numbers did not match those on the permit. *(AP/ Wide World Photos)*

Bell's adult children in 1991. Front row: Donald Dunbar Bell and Alice Adams Bell. Rear: Henry Curtis Bell. *(United Press International photo)*

TOP TEN REJECTED NAMES FOR KENTUCKY FRIED CHICKEN

10. Lifeless Bird Lumps

9. KFC and CPR

8. Hot Oily Hens

7. Greaseland

6. The You're-a-Little-Too-Late Petting Zoo

5. Heart Attack Helper

4. Jiffy Lube (already taken)

3. Home of the Soggy, Grease-Stained Bucket o' Fun

2. Food, Folks, and Fat

1. Artery Busters

TOP TEN THINGS OVERHEARD ON EARTH DAY

10. "Hey! After the concert let's trash the place!"

9. "It's the greenhouse effect, officer. That's why I'm not wearing pants."

8. "Who cares if it destroys the ozone? Thanks to aerosol cans, I can spell my name in cheese!"

7. "Look! I've carved 'Save the Whales' into this redwood!"

6. "Good news! June Allyson has switched to cloth diapers!"

5. "That's right. You get a nickel a can, Mr. Trump."

4. "Burning tires is bad for the ecosystem—but it adds a great smoky flavor to ham."

3. "Gimme a quarter." (New York City only)

2. "Once this land belonged to the Indians . . . that was before the Japanese."

1. "The corn dogs were better at Hands Across America."

TOP TEN REASONS THE BRITISH LOST THE COLONIES

10. Hard to shoot straight with sissified powdered wig falling in your eyes

9. Wanted to just lose New Jersey but got carried away

8. Colonists on steroids

7. Spent too much time guessing who's gay in the royal family

6. Their diet: tea and crumpets. Our diet: raw squirrel meat and whiskey.

5. Serious problems with snuff abuse

4. Lots of painful poking accidents trying to put on those pointy hats of theirs

3. We had Batman

2. Wanted to get first draft choice

1. Uninspiring battle cry: "Let's win this for our swishy inbred monarch!"

TOP TEN TALENTS OF THE CONTESTANTS IN THE MISS IRAQ PAGEANT

10. High-pitched shrieking

9. Getting plastic explosives through airport security

8. Withstanding the kick of a donkey

7. Making poison gas out of common household cleansers

6. Pointing to Mecca after being spun around three times blindfolded

5. Describing what they would look like in a swimsuit if they were permitted to wear one

4. Denouncing pork

3. Blowing self up in car in parking lot

2. Vogue-ing

1. Beating the crap out of Miss Kuwait

DICK TRACY'S TOP TEN
PET PEEVES

10. Two-way wrist radio keeps picking up Larry King

9. Waiting for Mumbles to order in a French restaurant

8. Wise guys who holler, "Hey! Where's the Batmobile?"

7. When McGruff the Crime Dog borrows trenchcoat and sheds in it

6. Still haven't figured out ending of "Twin Peaks"

5. Jack Lord always bragging about weather in Hawaii

4. People who tell off-color stories about J. Edgar Hoover

3. When Pruneface kids you about *Ishtar*

2. When fellow cops refer to wrist radio as "bracelet"

1. People who say "nucular" instead of "nuclear"

TOP TEN SIGNS THAT JIM BAKKER IS REHABILITATED

10. Can now remember six of the commandments

9. Has thrown out his Rolodex of preacher groupies

8. His prayers include less frequent use of the term "vacation home"

7. No longer shoplifts condoms

6. Openly admits his attraction to Tammy Faye may have been a passing clown fetish

5. Has told groups of visiting theologians, in all candor, "I am an incredible dork"

4. Has stopped writing love letters to Hugh Downs

3. Got *Sports Illustrated* subscription for the football phone—*not* the swimsuit issue

2. Now gleefully admits that yes, he does look like a frog

1. He's wearing pants again

DAN QUAYLE'S TOP TEN NEW YEAR'S RESOLUTIONS

10. Think of snappy comeback to Bentsen for that "You're no Kennedy" remark

9. Finally get it straight: Democrats are the donkey, Republicans the elephant

8. Get Marilyn's little dog to write a book the way Barbara Bush got hers to

7. Eat a zillion M&M's

6. So long, 8-tracks. Hello, cassettes!

5. Renew ties with family of ducks that raised him

4. When meeting foreign dignitaries, try not to crack up and say, "What a funny hat!"

3. Spend more time with imaginary friend "Leslie"

2. Catch Roadrunner

1. Learn to say "Sununu" without giggling

TOP TEN NEW YORK CITY THANKSGIVING TRADITIONS

10. Taking a hooker to the Mayflower Hotel

9. Go to supermarket, try to fit three frozen turkeys in your trenchcoat

8. Traveling over the river and through the woods to Grandmother's crack den

7. Dangle turkey neck out of pants

6. Get spot on roof of building for Macy's parade, try to spit on Santa

5. Free slivers of ham placed in taxi cab change slots

4. Fun Pilgrim hat drawn on all chalk body outlines

3. Family gathers at table, holds hands, and recites the Miranda warning

2. Turning off the Jets game after the first quarter

1. Finish your meal, loosen your belt, then doze off until the manager of the Sizzler calls the cops

TOP TEN CHANGES IN THE MUSTANG RANCH NOW THAT IT'S OWNED BY THE GOVERNMENT

10. Airbags installed in headboards of all beds

9. Popular "whipped cream" treatment now uses government surplus cheese

8. A simple half and half now involves hours of paperwork

7. Chipped beef on toast

6. Marion Barry once again interested in government work

5. Easygoing, low-pressure atmosphere maintained by experts from Postal Service

4. Etchings of naked women replaced by clown paintings by Gerald Ford

3. Name changed to Fort Dix

2. Main gate marked by giant billboard of pantsless Uncle Sam

1. T-shirts in gift shop say "I got screwed by the government"

TOP TEN SLOGANS FOR THE WORLD LEAGUE OF AMERICAN FOOTBALL

10. All our players have day jobs!

9. Plenty of good franchises still available!

8. You might see some snotty European break something!

7. Tired of watching overpaid, well-known, highly gifted athletes?

6. C'mon! We're trying to get enough people together for a "wave!"

5. If you half-close your eyes, it sort of looks like arena football!

4. See us now—before we're in Chapter 11!

3. You can't spell "waffle" without W-L-A-F

2. Because when somebody says, "Barcelona," "London," or "Frankfurt," you think *football!!*

1. No Steinbrenner!

TOP TEN WAYS TO GET HUSSEIN OUT OF KUWAIT

10. Ask really nicely

9. Tell Hussein he's won tickets to the Giants game. As soon as he sits down—nab him!

8. Threaten to tell his folks

7. Have phone company call every Iraqi soldier. Tell them they have to be home the next day between 8 and 5.

6. Explain to him that what he's done is wrong. Then bomb him back to the Stone Age.

5. Mention the old story about the place being haunted

4. Convince him it's the senseless, irrational thing to do

3. Creep him out by having CIA ventriloquists make his pets say stuff like "Get out of Kuwait"

2. Tell him you heard they were giving out fudge in Pakistan

1. Get Charles Bronson to "clean house"

TOP TEN LEAST POPULAR BRANDS OF CIGARETTES

10. Hint o' Lint 100's

9. Sleepy's Mattress-Flashers

8. Gee, Your Lungs Smell Terrific

7. Benson & Hedges Trimmings

6. Die-Before-Your-Kid-Goes-to-College Lights

5. L&M Turkish Prison Standards

4. Ozark Eddie's Mentholated Skeeter Chasers

3. Marion Barry "Extras"

2. Mr. Butt

1. Oscar Mayer Smokable Weenies

TOP TEN THINGS THAT WILL GET YOU AUDITED BY THE IRS

10. Using one of those "love" stamps for postage

9. Have taxes done by stupid, incompetent H. Block instead of by smart, reliable R. Block

8. Using the last name "Helmsley"

7. Calling IRS hotline and offering operator $1.50 a minute to talk dirty

6. Writing off hitchhiker buried in basement as dependent

5. In lieu of payment check, including handwritten coupon good for one "super-duper" backrub

4. Sending in pizza crusts instead of restaurant receipts

3. Writing off purchase of Tito Jackson album as charitable donation

2. Claiming hookers as medical expenses

1. Request filing extension for "until hell freezes over"

TOP TEN REJECTED HALF-TIME SHOWS FOR THE SUPER BOWL

10. "The 'Up with People' Kids Suffering from Really Bad Head Colds"

9. "The National Organization of Women Presents 'Victor Kiam, Go to Hell' "

8. "A Thousand Shirtless Drunk Guys in Rainbow Wigs"

7. "Vicious Dog Chases Frank Gifford Across the Field"

6. "Twenty-five Years of Super Bowl Groin Pulls"

5. "Open Mike Night"

4. "When Meat Rots"

3. "John Madden Tries to Do a Sit-up"

2. "The Golden Girls: Topless!"

1. "The Sounds of Recession"

TOP TEN SIGNS THAT YOUR BANK IS FAILING

10. Free handful of Chee•tos with every new account

9. They hand out calendars one month at a time

8. The security guard offers to walk you back to your office for five bucks

7. You overhear branch manager muttering to himself, "I wonder if you can eat squirrel?"

6. Free giveaway toaster is made by G.E.

5. Automatic teller machine replaced by fat guy with open carton of twenties

4. You glimpse inside the vault and notice it's stacked with empty soda bottles

3. When you deposit cash, a bank officer runs over, sticks it in his pocket, and dances around yelling, "Lordy, lordy! We're having biscuits tonight!"

2. You recognize some of the tellers as carnival people

1. They can't change a twenty

TED KENNEDY'S TOP TEN PARTY TIPS

10. Having a son or nephew around is a great ice-breaker with the younger babes

9. Flaming tumblers of Sambuca keep away the mosquitoes

8. Pretending to lose a contact lens is a terrific way to look up skirts

7. Make sure cocktail napkins have liability waiver on back

6. Wake up the kids after midnight for Jell-O shots

5. Mix Chivas and Slim-Fast: get drunk *and* lose weight

4. Two words: Wang Chung

3. Invite Supreme Court Justice David Souter—that guy is a party nut job!

2. Billy Dee Williams was right: Colt .45

1. Take off pants. Mingle.

TOP TEN RESEARCH PROJECTS AT CLOWN COLLEGE

10. The correlation of exploding cigars and facial abrasions

9. Seltzer versus soda water: Which is funnier?

8. Anti-gravity hair

7. Reducing carpool costs by traveling 28 to a car

6. Big shoes that are resistant to elephant manure

5. Can a cream pie's cholesterol be absorbed through the skin?

4. The Hubble telescope

3. Why chicks dig clowns

2. Prehistoric forerunners of the rubber weenie

1. Should steroids for the feet be banned?

TOP TEN SURPRISES IN
ROCKY V

10. Don King's nude scene

9. Eight sequences choreographed by Peter Allen

8. Rocky killed by Laura Palmer's father

7. Rocky's new manager Fred MacMurray puts Flubber in Rocky's gloves; Rocky knocks opponent to Mars

6. Mr. T? Gay as a French horn.

5. Rocky goes back into the ring and fights a younger, stronger opponent and even though he hasn't a chance in the world to beat him, Rocky digs down and musters all the courage and heart he can, and—you'll never believe this—wins anyway!

4. Lovable character Chewbacca dies

3. Weatherman Al Roker looks even bigger than last year (I'm sorry, that's one of the surprises in "Live at 5".)

2. That the referee didn't stop the series at *Rocky III*

1. You paid $7.50 to see it

TOP TEN THINGS THAT WILL GET YOU KICKED OUT OF IRAQ'S REPUBLICAN GUARD

10. Giggling during story time

9. Asking commander during inspection, "Are those Bugle Boy jeans?"

8. Blaring Barbra Streisand records in the barracks

7. Whenever enemy aircraft appears, dropping your gun and screaming like a woman

6. Wearing "Home of the Scud Missile" boxer shorts

5. Comments like "Wow! That Hussein guy is nuts!"

4. Holding membership in B'nai B'rith

3. Wearing those pajamas with feet

2. Double-dating with Arthur Kent

1. Laughing hysterically as you point to the sky and say, "Hey, look, everybody! More B-52's!"

TOP TEN SERIAL KILLER PET PEEVES

10. Police composite sketches that make you look ten years older than you really are

9. Hefty bags that leak

8. When you're hoping for a cool nickname like "Zodiac" or "Midnight Madman" and media gives you nickname "Tubby"

7. Crummy Ginsu knives they sell on TV that claim to stay sharp forever

6. When really expensive "night vision goggles" turn out to be just a scuba mask with red cellophane taped over glass

5. When you're a really *neat* serial killer and you have to move in with a really *messy* serial killer

4. It's always some neighbor you barely know who ends up yapping on the news about you being "a troubled loner"

3. Rarely have "Serial Killer Day" at the ballpark

2. When you finally meet somebody you really like, you always end up killing them

1. Movie *Silence of the Lambs* not as funny as the book

JOHN SUNUNU'S TOP TEN ETHICS VIOLATIONS

10. Used nuclear sub *Ticonderoga* to pick up carton of Luckies from Nantucket 7-Eleven

9. Used CIA technology to be 104th caller and win party weekend with Tesla

8. Altered driver's license to John "Sunoco" and tried to get free gas

7. Borrowed Fonzie's jacket from Smithsonian for Halloween party

6. Hocked original draft of Constitution at Bethesda pawnshop to buy a pair of golf slacks

5. Had presidential helicopter fly low over yard to trim his hedges

4. Had Quayle wash his car

3. Sneaking down to warehouse to eat government cheese

2. Midnight lap parties at the Lincoln Memorial

1. Acting weaselly in general

TOP TEN LEAST POPULAR TV DINNERS

10. Split Pea and Hamster

9. Swanson's Sweaty Man Dinner

8. Hot 'n' Hearty Microbe Casserole

7. Scorched Canadian Geese Extracted from Commercial Jet Engines

6. Al Sharpton's Veal Medallions

5. Jolly Green Giant's Assorted Elf Parts

4. I Can't Believe It's Not Perch!

3. Old-Fashioned Singed Tabby

2. John Gotti's Guys-Who-Crossed-Me Stew

1. Freak Show Sushi

TOP TEN WAYS FRANCE IS DEALING WITH GERMAN REUNIFICATION

10. Dialing 911

9. Installing speed bumps to slow Panzers down

8. Cutting bedsheets into convenient easy-to-wave white rectangles

7. Watching twice as many Jerry Lewis movies just to keep their spirits up

6. Stockpiling Blistex so they can kiss plenty of German butt

5. Printing up T-shirts that say "Don't shoot! I'm a collaborator!"

4. Going a really *really* long time without bathing

3. Suddenly acting all chummy with Chuck Norris

2. Practicing running backwards and blowing kisses

1. Developing top secret Stealth Cheese

TOP TEN SIGNS OF SPRING IN NEW YORK CITY

10. Crack dens take down storm windows

9. Dramatic increase in number of murders committed with gardening equipment

8. First robin of spring spotted in mouth of guy on D train

7. Lovely pastel colors used for chalk body outlines

6. Guys who usually take leaks in subway now take leaks on street

5. The Yankees are mathematically eliminated from American League pennant race

4. Tourists return for trial of guy who assaulted them last Christmas

3. Garbage collectors start going topless

2. Dog-sized rat emerges from subway and sees his shadow

1. Strangers begin moving into Dave Letterman's house

TOP TEN THINGS OVERHEARD AT THE CONGRESSIONAL PICNIC

10. "Sununu looks good in those bicycle pants."

9. "Just go behind the monument."

8. "More Cheez Whiz, Congressman?"

7. "I'm a member of the House of Representatives. Stop calling me 'Gopher'!"

6. "No, Mr. Vice President. You don't put the potato sack on your head."

5. "Isn't that Barney Frank and Bob Dole—slow dancing?"

4. "Look at all these weenies!"

3. "Mrs. Bush just finished her one hundredth deviled egg!"

2. "Put your pants on, Mr. Kennedy."

1. "Could I have another taxpayer-subsidized hamburger?"

TOP TEN PROVISIONS IN THE LOIS LANE/SUPERMAN PRE-NUPTIAL AGREEMENT

10. Joint custody of Jimmy Olsen

9. Won't wear same color tights at social gatherings

8. He has to clean up after his own super dog

7. No Kryptonite knickknacks

6. Lois must have Batman tattoo surgically removed

5. Superman must reverse Earth's rotation to go back in time and put toilet seat down

4. No use of heat vision around Ms. Lane's collection of decorative candles

3. Christmas Day with her folks; Protonium Eve with his

2. In the event of a divorce, Lois gets the Plaza Hotel

1. Superman prohibited from using X-ray vision at beach

TOP TEN LEAST POPULAR L. L. BEAN CATALOG ITEMS

10. The Al Sharpton Compass Medallion

9. The used Ace Bandage Hammock

8. Nasa's Hubble Binoculars

7. Fake Bear Vomit for Laughs on Camping Trips

6. Freeze-Dried Gristle

5. The Catheter-Equipped Waders

4. Inflatable Camping Partner

3. Shallow-Grave Shovel

2. Goose-Down Condoms

1. The Super-Slippery Ax

TOP TEN HIGHLIGHTS OF THE "C. EVERETT KOOP SHOW"

10. When that ridiculous fake beard started to fall off and he had to stick it back on

9. John Sununu trying to do a chin-up

8. Birth control demonstration with Super Dave Osborne driving Chevy pickup through giant condom

7. Suprise walk-on by Bob Hope during heart transplant operation

6. Tips on having safe sex with a Kennedy

5. The Claymation dancing liver spots

4. Marv Albert's reel of "Lab Test Bloopers"

3. The way he kept grabbing his crotch like Madonna

2. Sixty incoherent seconds with a malaria-crazed Andy Rooney

1. Magic trick where he pulled a live dove out of his beard

TOP TEN SIGNS YOU'VE GONE TO A BAD DOCTOR

10. His office is on the D train

9. Also promises to paint any car for $99.95

8. Last name Mengele

7. You're in what seems like a long, long tunnel and at the end is some light and the beckoning forms of loved ones who passed on years before

6. Giggles uncontrollably when he hears the word *penis*

5. Keeps asking, "Is somebody frying baloney?"

4. In middle of exam says, "Ever heard of a show called 'Totally Hidden Video'?"

3. Repeatedly asks, "What's that red stuff?"

2. Frequently wonders if you're getting enough fudge in your diet

1. After he asks you to cough, he says, "Okay, now my turn."

TOP TEN THINGS WE WILL MISS ABOUT SADDAM HUSSEIN

10. Cute way his nose wrinkles when he orders a Scud launch

9. The way he playfully teased us about making us swim in our own blood

8. His terrorist-studded Oscar-watching parties

7. Those funny commercials where he'd say, "Time to make the doughnuts"

6. The innocent way he'd look around, all confused, as everybody laughed at the mashed potatoes in his mustache

5. The way he made Donald Trump seem not so bad

4. Funny voice he'd use for sock puppet while ordering execution of family members

3. His "just folks" bunker hospitality

2. He gave bullies, thieves, and jerks a much-needed role model

1. The way you could make him jump a mile by popping a paper bag

TOP TEN WAYS McDONALD'S IS NOW MORE HEALTH CONSCIOUS

10. Ronald McDonald no longer spends night sleeping in salad bar

9. Happy Meals no longer include a pack of Luckies

8. When out of Shamrock Shakes, will no longer substitute mop water

7. Decorative bowls of mercury removed from tables

6. From now on, counter person will ask, "Would you like the name of a good heart specialist with that?"

5. Discontinuing "Find a Rusty Nail in Your Big Mac" promotional game

4. New combination salad dressing/sunblock

3. Employees must wash hands after patting down choking victims for wallet and jewelry

2. Mayor McCheese excused from duty at fry machine due to wet, hacking cough

1. Decided to drop Porksicles

TOP TEN LEAST POPULAR NEW YORK CITY STREET VENDORS

10. Deep-fried Sewer Bass

9. Calamari-Flavored Italian Ice

8. Hair Club for Men Emergency Glue Booth

7. Stunned Mouse in a Dixie Cup

6. Speedee Skin Graft

5. Your Photo Taken with a Cardboard Cutout of Federal Reserve Board Chairman Alan Greenspan

4. Fingerless Frank's Mystery Tacos

3. Old-fashioned Lint Cakes

2. Piping Hot Fried Dough Plus a Whack with a Hammer

1. Honey-Roasted Ticks

TOP TEN CAMPAIGN PROMISES BUSH HAS BROKEN

10. Birthday joyride on Stealth bomber for every U.S. citizen

 9. Go ten rounds with Dukakis at Trump Plaza

 8. To eat his own weight in birdseed twice a day

 7. Add mechanical-shark attraction to White House tour

 6. A pony for Quayle

 5. Add Golden Girls to Mount Rushmore

 4. To reduce gravity by 50 percent

 3. Vow to grow super-cool muttonchops

 2. Free tote bag to everybody who voted for him

 1. Nude Elvis postage stamp

TOP TEN THINGS OVERHEARD IN LINE FOR *KICKBOXER II*

10. "I hear there's lots of kickboxing in this one."

9. "If you didn't see Part One, you probably won't be able to follow it."

8. "It's a lot like *Star Wars*—only it doesn't take place in outer space and there's lots more kicking."

7. "Do me a favor and kick me a couple times to get me in the mood."

6. "Excuse me, Mrs. Onassis—but could you quit shoving?"

5. "I'll bet Julia Roberts broke up with Kiefer Sutherland 'cause he couldn't kickbox."

4. "So after I knocked over the vase and flowers, my mom said, 'No more kickboxing.' "

3. "It's adapted from the Henry James novel."

2. "Do you think *Kickboxer* could beat *Terminator*?"

1. "It's the best movie ever made about people kicking each other."

TOP TEN PROMOTIONAL SLOGANS FOR TAMPERED-WITH SUDAFED

10. Sudafed: I dare you

9. Comes in regular nonfatal, and now new fatal!

8. Kills bugs on contact

7. Sudafed—it rhymes with *dead*

6. Claus von Bülow liked it so much he bought the company!

5. Take a dance lesson with Arthur Murray

4. If Shirley MacLaine is right, you've got nothing to worry about

3. Sudafed—take me away!

2. If you're not dead in thirty minutes—the Sudafed's free!

1. No more food, no more folks, no more fun

TOP TEN WAYS DAVID SOUTER CELEBRATED HIS CONFIRMATION TO THE SUPREME COURT

10. Smiled for a few seconds, then went back to serious thoughts

 9. Bought Sandra Day O'Connor a robe from Victoria's Secret

 8. Marched into judicial supply store and announced, "The gavels are on me!"

 7. Talked to Nike about an endorsement deal

 6. Kicked Mom out of the house. Had girl over.

 5. Made paper hat out of U.S. Constitution, filled it with beer, put it on

 4. Paid his college dope-smoking buddies the rest of the hush money

 3. Ate his usual cottage cheese lunch off the chest of a thousand-dollar-a-night hooker

 2. Shouted "yee-haw!" while firing six-shooters into air

 1. Gave big wet kiss to Thurgood Marshall

TOP TEN SURPRISES IN THE ZACHARY TAYLOR AUTOPSY

10. Had bottlecaps and a license plate in his stomach

9. Wearing green blazer from PGA Masters Tournament

8. Pockets suffed with little soaps you get free from motels

7. Coffin contained perfectly preserved package of Velveeta

6. Let's just say Mrs. Taylor was a very lucky woman

5. Used Crest—but not new Crest with tartar-control gel

4. Currently has better memory than Reagan

3. Buried in a rainbow wig

2. There's some cocktail waitress in there with him

1. His nails are still salon-perfect

TOP TEN NEW JOBS FOR MILLI VANILLI

10. Open law firm of Jacoby, Meyers, Milli & Vanilli

9. Camp Counselors in Father Flanagan's Pretty Boys Town

8. Jamaican pickpockets in American Express commercial

7. Try to sell Ben and Jerry's on idea for "Milli Vanilla"

6. Cartoon pals to Chilly-Willy

5. Professional objects of scorn and ridicule for years to come

4. Selling "grit"

3. Even Newer Kids on the Block

2. Extremely groovy fry cooks

1. Who cares? Just so long as we don't hear from them ever again

TOP TEN SIGNS GORBACHEV IS ON THE VERGE OF A NERVOUS BREAKDOWN

10. At recent state dinner, kept goosing Belgian ambassador

9. Constantly calls *Time/LIFE* operators, chats for hours, and never orders anything

8. The other day, he told Lithuania it was "grounded"

7. Tried to get service in a 7-Eleven without shirt or shoes

6. Has put up huge poster of Jim Palmer in his office

5. Can suddenly understand everything Shirley MacLaine says

4. Opened discount electronics store and is selling things at prices so low he's practically giving them away

3. Thinks he has a red spot on his head

2. Keeps a dozen live tropical birds in his car

1. Shoots out TV every time Robert Goulet comes on

TOP TEN EFFECTS OF A MAJOR SOLAR FLARE

10. Brokaw does Nightly News with thick Italian accent

9. Grocery bag boys suffer incontinence

8. Bobby "The Brain" Heenan loses intellectual brilliance; must rely on brute force to defeat opponents

7. New York City cab drivers speak perfect English

6. Really bad NBC TV movie: *Solar Flare 2000*

5. Coca-Cola launches promotional tie-in

4. Top Ten Lists no longer seem funny

3. Don King's hair: no effect

2. Letter *p* no longer silent in the word *pneumonia*

1. G.E. light bulbs burn out faster than usual

TOP TEN REJECTED TITLES FOR REAGAN'S MEMOIRS

10. *Still Hazy After All These Years*

9. *Fall Asleep Anywhere, Anytime*

8. *How to Make Love to a Shrewish, Domineering First Lady*

7. *Shemp: My Favorite Stooge*

6. *The Ronald Colman Story*

5. *Nancy Reagan's Autobiography of Ronald Reagan*

4. *1001 Sam Donaldson Jokes*

3. *Uh*

2. *What? I'm Not Still President?*

1. *Hey, Hinckley—Pardon This!*

TOP TEN IRAQI BUMPER STICKERS

10. Don't tailgate: Car bomb on board

9. Have you hugged your hostage today?

8. If we could vote, I'd vote yes on Bond Issue 6

7. If chemical weapons are outlawed, only outlaws will have chemical weapons

6. I got my camel dunked at Raging Rapids Water Park

5. Baghdad Wolverines: 1986 Division Champions

4. Gay and proud of it

3. My other vehicle is a Soviet-Made T-72 tank

2. Don't like my driving? Call 1-800-EAT-PORK

1. Honk if you still have hands

TOP TEN WAYS BUSH COULD BLOW IT IN '92

10. Unloads Barbara for a nineteen-year-old male prostitute

9. Gets really sick during White House ceremony; throws up on Super Bowl winners

8. Opens fire with an Uzi on a tour group

7. Guest stars on "Matlock"; shoots Andy Griffith in face

6. It is revealed he bet against the U.S. in the Gulf War

5. Decides to grow stylish Hitler mustache

4. Goes on "Jeopardy!"; loses $82,000 in taxpayers' money

3. Chooses Quayle as his running mate

2. Gets careless about secret family in West Virginia

1. Appears on "Donahue" as "Debbie Bush"

TOP TEN BIG NEWS STORIES BURIED ON THE BACK PAGES OF THE NEWSPAPER

10. Walter Mondale trapped in Texas well

9. New drug allows Cocoa Puffs bird to calmly consume Cocoa Puffs

8. Hitler found alive, managing Milwaukee Radio Shack

7. Brothers from rock group Nelson wed in courthouse mix-up

6. Pete Rose's dog banned from Baseball Players' Dog Hall of Fame

5. Early Shatner hairpiece fetches record million at Sotheby's auction

4. Canada massing troops on Alaskan border

3. Congress ratifies new amendment: *Soup* to be spelled "S-U-P-E"

2. Super Bowl played early; six-hour game ends in scoreless tie

1. New Monkees reunited

TOP TEN LEAST INTERESTING ACADEMY AWARDS CATEGORIES

10. Best-Looking Rubber Ears

9. Best Banjo Accompaniment to a Reckless-Driving Scene

8. Most Flagrant Lingering Shot of a Brand-Name Product

7. Most Arbitrary Snit by a Supporting Actress

6. Best Straight Costume Designer

5. Tastiest Petrolium-Based Butter Substitute Used in Lobby Concession Stand

4. Best Best Boy

3. Shirley MacLaine Previous Lifetime Achievement Award

2. Best Hair on Back

1. Film Most Likely to Be Rejected—by the Airlines

TOP TEN COOL THINGS ABOUT BORIS YELTSIN

10. Once won air-guitar contest at Moscow Houlihan's

9. Brews his own potato beer in a bucket in the attic

8. Can start up jukebox just by rapping it with his fist

7. Knows where Gorbachev is really ticklish

6. On a bet, once ate ten thousand M&M's

5. Cracks up Politburo by putting on a leather jacket and doing his Boris "Dice" Yeltsin routine

4. *Yeltsin* is Russian word for *Retsin*

3. Moonlights in Mayor McCheese costume at Red Square McDonald's

2. The rocket-powered Yeltsinmobile

1. Can drink Ted Kennedy under the table

NASA'S TOP TEN EXCUSES FOR THE HUBBLE TELESCOPE MALFUNCTIONS

10. The guy at Sears promised it would work fine

9. Some kids on Earth must be fooling around with a garage-door opener

8. There's a little doohickey rubbing against the part that looks kind of like a cowboy hat

7. See if *you* can think straight after twelve days of drinking Tang

6. Bum with Squeegee smeared lens at red light

5. Blueprints drawn up by that "Hey, Vern!" guy

4. Those damn raccoons!

3. Shouldn't have used G.E. components

2. Ran out of quarters

1. Race of super-evolved galactic beings are screwing with us

TOP TEN REASONS MILLS COLLEGE GIRLS DON'T WANT MEN ATTENDING

10. No more going to library topless

9. Annual production of Chekhov's *Three Sisters* would be replaced by three-day Stooge-a-thon

8. Football team has perfect 0–452 record

7. Guys often whoop and holler when words like *breast* appear in sensitive poetry

6. There's going to be some loser named Ned who keeps asking everyone out

5. They might try to free the men we use in our science projects

4. We're shy

3. Afraid cafeteria walls will be covered with "Dukes of Hazzard" posters

2. Less beer for the rest of us

1. They tend to spit a lot

TOP TEN SIGNS YOU'VE GONE TO A BAD FUNERAL DIRECTOR

10. He's wearing a paper trainee hat

9. Hawaiian Punch used for embalming fluid

8. Hearse has Domino's logo on side; on way to cemetery they drop off a couple of pizzas

7. Tells you, "I can't help this man. He's dead."

6. Asks if you want cremation to be Original or Crispy

5. Gives out souvenir T-shirts reading "My beloved spouse passed away and all I got was this lousy T-shirt"

4. Gives you business card for his secondhand eyeglass and denture shop

3. He tells bereaved "I'm pretty sure your uncle's in hell by now"

2. Two days after the funeral you see the deceased alive again doing yardwork for the funeral director

1. Replaces ashes of loved one with Folgers crystals

TOP TEN ITEMS FROM THE NORTH POLE POLICE BLOTTER

10. Two white male elves caught shoplifting condoms at Pay 'n' Save

9. Santa stabbed for his jacket

8. Broke up domestic squabble between Dancer and Prancer

7. Female polar bear at disco allegedly fondled by Mike Tyson

6. Frosty the Snowman caught taking a leak in subway; claimed he was just "melting"

5. Unidentified three-foot, six-inch male wearing pointy cap and bells on shoes shot dead while dining at local Italian eatery

4. Santa's sleigh found completely stripped five thousand miles away on Cross-Bronx Expressway

3. Computer hacker released to custody of parents after illegally inserting name onto "nice" list

2. Issued warning at frat party to turn down the Burl Ives records

1. Arrested thirty-five-year-old white male who refused to get off Santa's lap

TOP TEN APPROVED EXERCISES FOR PRESIDENT BUSH

10. Panda wrestling at the National Zoo

9. Air guitar

8. Doing the hula to Neil Diamond records

7. Running to top of Capitol steps, then jumping up and down like Rocky

6. Joining Secret Service in game of keep-away with Quayle's hat

5. Looking for leftover Easter eggs on White House lawn

4. Crushing beer cans against his forehead

3. Exercise the ol' pocket veto, if you know what I mean

2. Sweatin' to the Oldies

1. Bar-hopping with Ted Kennedy

TOP TEN WAYS QADHAFI CAN REGAIN THE TITLE OF WORLD'S MOST INSANE LEADER

10. Eat his own foot in front of *Newsweek* reporter

9. Hijackings every hour on the hour

8. Put inflated surgical glove on his head at press conference

7. Buy stock in Eastern Airlines

6. Go on cross-country car trip with Joe Piscopo; ask, "Do you do impressions?"

5. Continually ask himself, "What would Curly do?"

4. Appoint Quayle vice president

3. Appear before U.N. General Assembly and consume an entire can of Crisco in one minute

2. Marry Cher

1. Take self hostage

TOP TEN SLOGANS FOR THE 1992 DEMOCRATIC CONVENTION

10. Okay. We're serious this time.

9. Guys stay free in Barney Frank's hotel room

8. We're the Cleveland Indians of politics

7. Watch the fun as Gerald Ford shows up by mistake

6. One of *our* presidents dated Marilyn Monroe

5. We're digging up Lyndon Johnson and we're running him again

4. Polls, schmolls!

3. We're the party without Quayle

2. We may date dippy blondes, drink excessively, and harbor at-home male prostitution rings, but we'd never lie about taxes, which, by the way, we plan to raise

1. Just wait till '96!

DAN QUAYLE'S TOP TEN COMPLAINTS ABOUT FRANCE

10. Virtually impossible to find a box of Cap'n Crunch

9. Long lines at Jerry Lewis movies

8. French people speak some kind of weird moon-man language

7. Water fountain in bathroom must be designed for midgets

6. Snobby French won't elect *their* government officials unless they have qualifications of some kind

5. After all the hype about "Big Ben," it's nowhere to be found

4. Doesn't know how many hours ahead to set Mickey's hands

3. The Happy Meals taste different

2. Primitive cheese slices not individually wrapped

1. Everyone keeps referring to him as "Le Bonehead"

TOP TEN THINGS BUSH LIKES ABOUT SUPREME COURT JUSTICE DAVID SOUTER

10. Wears the same size robe as Brennan

9. The funny way he says "Whoa! Order in the court!" after he belches

8. Only federal judge who hasn't hit on Barbara Bush

7. Millie likes him

6. The colorful clothes he wears and the way the sunlight plays upon his hair

5. Helped Dan Quayle beat the rap after he killed a guy at the dog track

4. Heard he did magic tricks like the judge on "Night Court"

3. His Trans-am has a bitchin' sound system

2. He has the figure for bicycle pants

1. Once beat the crap out of Jacoby *and* Meyers

TOP TEN SHOCKING REVELATIONS IN KITTY KELLEY'S BIOGRAPHY OF DAVE THOMAS, FOUNDER OF WENDY'S

10. Like Sinatra, he had White House affair with Nancy Reagan

9. Once ate a Wendy's double cheeseburger off a hooker's chest

8. Anyone opposing him could wake up to find a greasy burger patty in their bed

7. Little girl who was original Wendy in logo now a grown-up cocktail waitress in Houston strip joint

6. Once called John Gotti to ask how much it would cost to "take care of" Ronald McDonald

5. Dropped pants at board meetings whenever someone said, "Where's the beef?"

4. Claims Prince's song "Raspberry Beret" is actually about him

3. Routinely pulls up to a Burger King drive-through intercom, orders 500 burgers, then backs out

2. Once shot out TV set when Colonel Sanders came on

1. Really enjoys leaning against shake machine because it vibrates so much

TOP TEN SURPRISES IN BUSH'S STATE-OF-THE-UNION ADDRESS

10. First president to address joint session of Congress shirtless

9. Refreshing decision to read speech in comical Yiddish accent

8. Extracting one of his own teeth with pair of pliers

7. Secret Service's excessive use of force in subduing Energizer bunny

6. Way Jack Kemp and Elizabeth Dole openly made out all during speech

5. Entertaining way his puppet pal Koko announced tax increases while president drank a glass of water

4. Offer to sell, at Blue Book value, his old *Air Force One*

3. His assertion that he's a little girl trapped in a man's body

2. Apology for unprovoked air strike against Montreal

1. Concluding speech by saying, "Time to make the doughnuts"

TOP TEN THINGS OVERHEARD AT THE ACADEMY AWARDS

10. "Isn't that Meryl Streep with Bobby 'The Brain' Heenan?"

9. "We're all meeting later at Bob Denver's house for Pizza Rolls and Sprite!"

8. "Uh-oh. The guys from Price Waterhouse are talking to Pete Rose."

7. "Yes, Mr. Ebert, I am gonna finish this sandwich."

6. "Excuse me, Mr. Nicholson, you dropped this million-dollar bill."

5. "It's a crime they snubbed that 'Hey, Vern!' guy again."

4. "Hey! Get your hand out of—oh, Mr. Beatty, so nice to meet you."

3. "Wow! The soap cakes in the urinal are shaped like Oscar!"

2. "Hey, look! The Little Mermaid is drunk!"

1. "I'm Dorothy Chandler—I'm mad as hell and I want you all out of my pavilion *right now!*"

ARNOLD SCHWARZENEGGER'S TOP TEN REJECTED MOVIE LINES

10. "My, what a lovely lace doily!"

9. "Oww! A paper cut!"

8. "Man oh man, do I love fudge!"

7. "It's not a purse. It's a utility bag."

6. "Do you have any of those 'ouchless' Band-Aids?"

5. "Can you please open this jar of olives for me?"

4. "Time to make the doughnuts, you *bastard!*"

3. "Can you just let me keep my credit cards?"

2. "Help me, Letterman! Help me!"

1. "Who else loves show tunes?"

TOP TEN REVELATIONS IN THE NEW MADONNA MOVIE *TRUTH OR DARE*

10. Was kicked out of *Up with People* as a teenager for grabbing herself during halftime show

9. We think that maybe she sometimes dyes her hair

8. She invented the auto air freshener

7. Inner-ear problems mean she has to wear special iron shoes for balance

6. Fire marshal once closed down her bedroom for overcrowding

5. Metal brassiere handy for opening long-neck Buds

4. Opening act on the Blonde Ambition tour: Buddy Hackett

3. Warren Beatty is only four foot ten

2. She's actually a painfully shy recluse who will do anything to avoid media attention

1. She once slept with Nancy Reagan

TOP TEN SIGNS YOUR NEIGHBOR IS A SERIAL KILLER

10. Overheard muttering to himself, "Damn lying squirrels!"

9. Wonders if his front lawn landscaping would impress Jodie Foster

8. Flashing neon sign on his roof reads DRIFTERS WELCOME

7. Since he moved to town, the paper's obituary section has expanded to four pages

6. Often selling Domino's Pizza uniforms at yard sales

5. Always says, "Let's see what else is on" whenever "America's Most Wanted" starts

4. You feel perfectly happy after killing one person, but he insists on killing more

3. Claims to be engaged to Kaye Ballard

2. Two words: swastika pajamas

1. Thinks he's the Vern that the "Hey, Vern" guy is talking to

TOP TEN HIGHLIGHTS FROM ESPN'S "SPORTSCENTER"

10. Heated round-table discussion: "Why Do Ballplayers Scratch Themselves?"

9. Inspiring segment: "Monster Trucks and the Men Who Lube Them"

8. Strangely fascinating slow-motion footage of Don Zimmer doing half gainer from the high board

7. Chris Berman's on-air proposal to Morganna the Kissing Bandit

6. Scoring tips from Ted Kennedy

5. Display of items found in stadium drinking fountains

4. When the fat film critic and the skinny film critic argue

3. During the Final Four recap Dick Vitale gets excited and swallows his tongue

2. Tommy Lasorda chugs gallon of Slim-Fast; loses 20 pounds on camera

1. Regular feature: "Groin-Pull Roundup"

TOP TEN WAYS TO SPEND THE EXTRA HOUR OF DAYLIGHT SAVINGS

10. Twenty three-minute eggs

9. Write *Police Academy* sequels 7 through 15

8. A wagonload of microwave waffles

7. Tell your family you love them (#7 has been brought to you by the Church of Jesus Christ of Latter-Day Saints)

6. Try on every pair of pants in your closet as you yell out the window, "They fit!"

5. Whittle

4. Memorize lyrics to "American Pie"

3. Call *Time/LIFE*. Hit on Judy the Operator.

2. Train your monkey to ride one of those little tricycles

1. Shampoo, rinse, repeat. Shampoo, rinse, repeat. Shampoo, rinse, repeat.

TOP TEN ITEMS CUT FROM THE ORIGINAL DECLARATION OF INDEPENDENCE

10. Request that the British keep New Jersey

9. P.S. from John Hancock: "Have a bitchin' summer"

8. Gratuitous reference to King George as "wig-wearing crumpet monkey"

7. Statement: Good-bye, fish and chips. Hello, Colonel Sanders.

6. Gag signature of Sonny Bono

5. Tear-off coupons good for discount at Philadelphia ale house

4. Promise to paint any car for $99.95

3. Demand for more rock, less talk

2. To show there are no hard feelings, please find enclosed a package of Vermont maple candy

1. Inalienable right to the pursuit of life, liberty, and leggy supermodels

TOP TEN THINGS (BESIDES GIVING UP FATTY FOODS) THAT WILL ADD FOUR MONTHS TO YOUR LIFE

10. Put suicide machine in reverse

9. Not giving the finger to Mr. Gotti's limo after he cuts you off

8. Dot your *i*'s with a smiley face

7. Averting your eyes whenever the Hamburger Helper Hand appears on TV

6. Unwrap gum completely before chewing

5. Being able to outrun the Los Angeles Police Department

4. Set yourself a goal: "I'm going to live four months longer than I normally would." Stick to it.

3. MCI instead of AT&T

2. Break into drugstore and eat all the medicine

1. New crack lite!

TOP TEN CANADIAN NICKNAMES FOR AMERICANS

10. Skinny Bacon Lovers

9. Gretskynappers

8. Continent Hogs

7. Un-Mounties

6. Surfboard-Riding Barbarians

5. Individually Wrapped Cheese Slice Junkies

4. Upper Mexicans

3. Pizza-Gorged Convertible Jockeys

2. Star-Spangled Sissy Boys

1. Puckstops

TOP TEN SIGNS SUNUNU IS ABOUT TO BE FIRED

10. His desk has been moved out by the dumpster

9. No longer gets to sit next to the President at puppet shows

8. White House paperboy asked if he could get his Christmas tip early

7. "I'm with Sununu" T-shirts removed from gift shop

6. During Cabinet meeting, Bush says, "I thought we fired your ass months ago"

5. When introduced to him, Boris Yeltsin said, "You the guy they're losing?"

4. In 1560 Nostradamus wrote, "A fat guy with a funny name will fly for free and get fired"

3. Jack Kemp said he could get him a tryout with the World League of American Football

2. Recently asked to appear on "Donahue" show about chiefs of staff who've been let go

1. Even Quayle won't give him the time of day

TOP TEN LEAST POPULAR BOY SCOUT MERIT BADGES

10. Spit Craft

9. Sitting in Fire

8. Judy Garland Lore

7. Police Informant

6. Shallow-Grave Maintenance

5. Afternoon with Linda Lavin

4. Trouser Tenting

3. Animal Waste Identification

2. Heimliching Squirrels

1. Toe Dancing

TOP TEN LITTLE TASKS FOR THE REUNITED GERMANY

10. Decide which picture of Elvis goes on the new 50-mark note

9. Remove phrase "East Germany blows" from national anthem

8. Send in change-of-address cards to wrestling magazines

7. Negotiate mutually agreeable license-plate slogan

6. Package more loose rocks as "Pieces of the Berlin Wall" for gullible American tourists

5. Retrieve plans for Fourth Reich from Swiss safe deposit box

4. Figure out whether Miss West Germany or Miss East Germany gets to go to the Miss Universe Pageant

3. Thank Roy Clark for orchestrating this whole reunification thing

2. Finish erasing giant white dotted line at border

1. Practice saying "We're going to Disney World!"

TOP TEN UNSUCCESSFUL LAMBADA MOVIES

10. *An Officer and a Lambada Instructor*

9. *Lambada: The Forbidden Phony-Baloney Fake Fad*

8. *Star Trek VI: Lambada!*

7. *Raymond Burr's Lambada in 3-D*

6. *Lambada: It's Spanish for "Polka"*

5. *Zorro Acts Swishy*

4. *Arnold Schwarzenegger Is the Lambadinator*

3. *The Triple A Presents: Defensive Driving the Lambada Way*

2. *Godzillambada*

1. *Lambada: The Dance No One's Actually Doing*

ANNOUNCER BILL WENDELL'S TOP TEN FAVORITE WORDS TO PRONOUNCE

10. Rotisserie

9. Diphtheria

8. Skink

7. Thick-a-licious

6. Salve

5. Tuber

4. Fahrvergnügen

3. Mellencamp

2. Ringworm

1. Weiner

TOP TEN THINGS OVERHEARD AT TRUMP'S TAJ MAHAL IN ATLANTIC CITY

10. "I wonder if we'll catch a glimpse of the reclusive Mr. Trump?"

9. "Honey, keep playing this slot for me while I take a leak."

8. "I'm sorry, sir. The do-over rule does not apply to blackjack."

7. "Of course your credit's good here, Mr. Rose."

6. "Security! Security! Ivana on level five!"

5. "Merciful Mother of God! With a single turn of the wheel—my life savings . . . *gone!*"

4. "Which way to the Trump Toilet?"

3. "I'm afraid we don't have a Yahtzee table, Mr. Quayle."

2. "Wow! I didn't know David Letterman could sing!"

1. "I'm in Taj Ma-*hell!*"

TOP TEN MORE REASONS WHY THIS BOOK IS BETTER THAN DAVE LETTERMAN'S TV SHOW

10. No phony-baloney actors and actresses plugging their piece-of-crap movies

9. Easier to swat away killer bees with paperback

8. If you're carrying it in your pocket and get shot with a small-caliber bullet from 500 yards away—*it could save your life!*

7. Dave's incessant whining edited out

6. Virtually no chance of Richard Simmons suddenly appearing in book

5. Introduction of typeset page sure to revolutionize medieval Europe

4. Book contains answers to written portion of your state's driving test

3. Book costs money. TV show given away free (our perspective only).

2. Harder for G.E. pinheads to louse up book

1. Book dedicated to *you*; TV show dedicated to a poodle that once saved Dave's life

TOP TEN GOOD THINGS ABOUT STEINBRENNER NOW THAT HE'S GONE

10. His pink slips had smiley faces on them

9. Never considered hiring guy in a chicken suit

8. Exhales carbon dioxide, which is needed by plants

7. Except for maybe six or seven times, never fired a manager on Christmas

6. Every day for past seventeen and a half years he has left flowers on the grave of Babe Ruth's favorite hooker

5. Once drank five-gallon drum of that nacho cheese stuff

4. Usually rewinds video rental

3. Makes Pete Rose feel better about himself

2. He personally blew up those inflatable bat souvenirs before each home game

1. Provides an inspiring role model for bullying crybabies everywhere

TOP TEN JFK, JR. EXCUSES FOR FAILING NEW YORK BAR EXAM A SECOND TIME

10. Should have actually answered essay questions instead of just writing "I'm a Kennedy"

9. Tutor Arnold Schwarzenegger over-emphasized the bench press

8. Thought answers had to be in form of a question

7. Took Uncle Ted's advice—but guy next to me was really dumb

6. Confused by typo; spent months pre-paring for *bra* exam

5. Didn't want to spoil inevitable tabloid headline "Hunk Flunks"

4. Caught glimpse of self in reflective sur-face and was unable to look away

3. Two words: sympathy tail

2. Afraid passing grade would mean talk-ing to Doug Llewelyn

1. Thought there'd be a relaxing "cock-tail and makeout break" midway through exam

TOP TEN WORDS USED LEAST IN THE BIBLE

10. Perky

9. Fudge-a-licious

8. Rootin'-tootin'

7. Buttinsky

6. Schweppervescence

5. Mall Bunny

4. Gas-guzzling

3. Yankee fan

2. *Boinnnng!*

1. Slap-happy

TOP TEN SURPRISES IN THE LONG-SECRET KRUSHCHEV INTERVIEW TAPES

10. Rosenbergs also gave KGB formula for McDonald's secret sauce

9. Started Cuban missile crisis to impress Kim Novak

8. Instigated long-term Soviet plan to destabilize New York Yankees' management

7. First documented use of phrase "It's Hammertime!"

6. Castro? Gay as a French trombone

5. Played backward, can hear message "Turnips are groovy"

4. Had nickname for each of his facial warts

3. Bonus: 30 minutes of his proven "Stop Smoking Now" technique

2. Claimed to be the fifth Beatle

1. Most frightening moment in his life: seeing Brezhnev naked

TOP TEN THINGS DAN QUAYLE MUST DO BEFORE OUR NEXT SUMMIT WITH THE SOVIETS

10. Make cardboard sign that reads "Gorbachev" to hold when he picks him up at airport

9. Bake the Soviet president a really cool cake in the shape of a race car

8. Look at hundreds of photos of guys with red spots on their heads until he no longer giggles

7. Try to find out best Chernobyl jokes just to break the ice

6. Learn to say, "Hi, I'm a bonehead" in Russian

5. Buy a new hand buzzer

4. Hitchhike to South Carolina to load up on fireworks

3. Confirm which countries are in NATO, which in Klingon Empire

2. Call his dad to see if he can get him out of going

1. Practice his curtsy

TOP TEN REASONS IRAQ WANTS AN ATOMIC BOMB

10. To impress the babes

9. Already spent a lot of money on a beautiful leather atomic bomb case

8. It'll bring in the tourists

7. Tired of being treated like a second-rate New Jersey

6. Just in case Liza Minnelli gets one

5. To get Syria to turn down the damn music

4. Conventional warfare went out with bell-bottoms

3. Need it to build really big swimming pool

2. For when some son of a bitch in a Porsche cuts us off on the freeway

1. Hey! We're a bunch of lunatics who want to destroy the world—so *sue* us!

TOP TEN LITTLE-KNOWN FACTS ABOUT CLARENCE THOMAS

10. Has two first names

9. Once reprimanded for using his gavel to tenderize veal

8. Sees appointment to Supreme Court as stepping stone to meeting Paula Abdul

7. Sent a man to jail in 1985 for eating pudding with a straw

6. Once, while handing down a verdict, coined the phrase "rat's ass"

5. Wrestles under name of "The Georgia Cyclone"

4. His legal writings make frequent reference to special episodes of "Kate & Allie"

3. Has named his nine poodles after Supreme Court justices

2. Designs his own robes

1. Loves Jacoby; hates Myers

TOP TEN REASONS
SHEVARDNADZE
RESIGNED

10. Didn't want to buy Christmas gifts for all the other guys in the Politburo

9. Offered chance to be opening act for Yakov Smirnoff

8. Got a good deal on a house in Chernobyl

7. It was revealed he lip-synched his last album

6. Strangely found himself increasingly attracted to Gorbachev

5. Kremlin couldn't match offer from the Dodgers

4. As Soviet Foreign Minister, he was not allowed to date Russian contestants in Miss Universe Pageant

3. Decided to follow the Grateful Dead full time

2. Got hit on head with bowling ball; now he thinks he's Ralph Kramden

1. Found out there was more chance for advancement at Moscow McDonald's

TOP TEN OTHER MARY HART SIDE EFFECTS

10. Hairdo interferes with satellite communications

9. Giggle induces skin rash in laboratory mice

8. Rapid blinking causes Roger Ebert to give a thumbs-up when he meant to give a thumbs-down

7. Her hiccups get owls "hot"

6. Every time she changes her oil, the Cleveland Indians win

5. Close proximity causes dopey grin (John Tesh only)

4. Laughter causes McDLT hot side to become cold, cold side to become hot

3. Her Las Vegas show provokes sudden urge to get your money back

2. That volcano in the Philippines

1. Perfume sets off smoke alarms

TOP TEN THINGS DENNIS THATCHER WILL MISS ABOUT HIS WIFE BEING PRIME MINISTER

10. All those men in powdered wigs hanging around

9. All the free samples from the Wham-O company

8. During summits, getting his hair done with Mrs. Mitterand

7. Taking the lift up to the flat or the pram or the telly or whatever the hell they call it

6. Winning fortune in bar bets by claiming he could screw the Prime Minister

5. Those impressive "Number Ten Downing Street" matchbooks he got to carry around

4. Going through Winston Churchill's collection of old *Playboy*s up in the attic

3. Those Saturday nights when he and Maggie would finish entire bottle of Jack Daniel's and then start making up some laws

2. Weekly saunas with Benny Hill

1. The admiration of unemployed, free-loading husbands everywhere

TOP TEN TIPS FOR KEEPING YOUR HUSBAND HAPPY (FROM THE WIVES OF MIDDLE EAST TERRORISTS)

10. Assure him he's just as maniacal as the day you first met

9. Leave little notes in his holster

8. Don't put out for hostages

7. Tell him you look like Michelle Pfeiffer. Never take your veil off.

6. Double-date with the Qaddafis

5. Second honeymoon in Beirut

4. Always offer to go first through a minefield

3. When bowling, keep telling him, "Boy those pins really fly when you hit them!"

2. Lull in your love life? Blow up a car.

1. Goat casserole—and plenty of it

TOP TEN WAYS GORBACHEV WILL SPEND HIS RAISE

10. Buy Hallmark's nicest "Let's Be Friends" card for Lithuania

9. Go nuts at the Gap

8. Get matching tattoo on other side of forehead

7. Take bus to Atlantic City and play some serious slots

6. Start dating Marla Maples

5. He's going to Disneyworld!

4. Switch from Slim-Fast to the more expensive *Ultra* Slim-Fast

3. Underwear

2. Can finally say he *would* like fries with that

1. Make it May Day *every* day!

TOP TEN KEEBLER ELF EUPHEMISMS FOR DEATH

10. Bit the big morsel

9. Failed his freshness test

8. On the cooling rack

7. Bought the Pepperidge Farm

6. Gone to aisle three

5. Creamy casket filling

4. Owl bait

3. Super-fudge-a-riffically-dead

2. Overbaked

1. Somebody get the Mini-Vac!

TOP TEN DOG THOUGHTS

10. "I could've *sworn* I heard the can opener."

9. "Why doesn't the government do something about mange?"

8. "Is there something I'm not getting about Norm Crosby?"

7. "I wonder if Toto was gay?"

6. "Mmm . . . that filthy standing water sure hits the spot!"

5. "Hey—no kidding, I'm *sure* that's the can opener."

4. "I still miss Lorne Greene."

3. "Would we dogs have built a vast and complex civilization of our own if we weren't distracted by our ability to lick ourselves?"

2. "Please, oh, please, oh, *please* let that be the can opener."

1. "If there's a God, how can He allow neutering?"

The "LATE NIGHT WITH DAVID LETTERMAN" BOOK of TOP TEN LISTS

TOP TEN REASONS TO BUY THIS BOOK

10) Serves as a handy coaster for two jumbo beverages

9) Plentiful misprints sure to make it a valuable collector's item

8) Ideal for really easy book report

7) Everything you need to know to pilot your own jumbo jet

6) Randomly selected page numbers could include winning lottery combinations

5) You're mentioned on page 43

4) Paper made from criminal trees which deserved to die

3) Sure to impress the babes

2) This is the very last copy in existence

1) *Damn it!* It's about time you did something for *you!*

Required reading for anyone interested in things that come in bunches of ten!

Also available now in paperback from

POCKET
BOOKS